CONTENTS

Ships in Focus Publications
Correspondence and editorial:
Roy Fenton
18 Durrington Avenue
London SW20 8NT
020 8879 3527
rfenton@rfenton.demon.co.uk

Orders and photographic:
John & Marion Clarkson
18 Franklands, Longton
Preston PR4 5PD
01772 612855
sales@shipsinfocus.co.uk

Printed by Amadeus Press Ltd.,
Cleckheaton, Yorkshire.
Designed by Hugh Smallwood, John
Clarkson and Roy Fenton.
SHIPS IN FOCUS RECORD
ISBN 1 901703 76 2

SHIPS IN FOCUS
March 2

The strong photographic content of this journal raises the question of how photographs are credited. Those readers who tell us they read every word in 'Record' may have noticed that here, and in our other publications such as our recent 'SD14: The Full Story', we have begun to extend the acknowledgements at the end of our captions to photographs. The thinking is that both the supplier of the print and the photographer deserve recognition. The copyright is with the photographer and - where known - he or she will get the first credit. The supplier (usually a collector) has acquired, conserved and filed the print or slide, and then gone to the trouble of looking it out and sending it to us, and he (or she) will also get a credit, but in second place. Without both these people, we would not be able to provide the photographic coverage that is an important part of 'Record'.

In applying the above principles some practical difficulties may be encountered. In some cases, it is not possible to identify the photographer: a minority of prints have no name stamped or written on the back. Sometimes the style of the photograph, the print itself, or the background may leave no doubt whose work it is. For instance, Basil Feilden's shots are instantly recognisable, even when they do not carry his name. Another problem is where negatives change hands. The negative collection of the late Alex Duncan, for example, is a particularly heterogenous one, with no indication on the negative bag of who took the photograph, though again some photographer's work is readily identifiable. When selecting photographs for publication it is amusing to find two views of a ship, taken perhaps only seconds apart, but credited to different individuals. The usual explanation is that a photographer took several shots and then one was sold to or swapped with another photographer or collector. In the case of Preston photographs, however, the reason for discovering two not-quite identical photos of the same ship on the same occasion is that Harry Stewart and Douglas Cochrane were standing side by side taking them!

Despite these difficulties, we shall endeavour to identify the taker of the shot as well as the supplier when possible, and our readers are encouraged to let us know if anyone's work goes uncredited. Whilst writing this it was noticed that the excellent 'Hudson Shipping' by Graham Atkinson and published by Bernard McCall has adopted a similar style of acknowledgement. We would urge other publishers to do likewise, and to ensure that 'Author's collection' or 'Company archives' is the credit of last resort.
John Clarkson   Roy Fenton

SUBSCRIPTION RATES FOR RECORD
Readers may start their subscription with any issue, and are welcome to backdate it to receive any previous issues.

	3 issues	4 issues
UK	£23	£31
Europe (airmail)	£25	£34
Rest of world (surface)	£25	£34
Rest of world (airmail)	£30	£40

In Gallions Reach on 7th March 1936, *Sun II* assists *Marquesa*: see pages 66-73. *[R.A. Snook, Roy Fenton collection]*

Fleet in Focus
THE FURNESS WITHY - HOULDER BROTHERS LINK
Part 2
D.H. Johnzon

Baronesa sailing from Liverpool. *[John McRoberts, D.H.Johnzon collection]*

The 1918 quartet

Baronesa, Duquesa, Princesa and *Marquesa*, each from a different shipyard (see fleet list), entered service in April, May and July 1918. The fitting of topmasts to fore and main had been left until hostilities ceased, whilst at least one of them - *Marquesa* - first appeared, rather late in the day, in dazzle paintwork. The *Marquesa*, in fact, differed from the rest in that, being minus a full boat deck, her boats were at bridge deck level. In all other respects these ships were very similar, following the pattern set by the *Condesa*; their capacity for refrigerated cargo averaging 480,000 cubic feet.

Sailors, it is often said, tend to be superstitious, and the claim of any who served in the *Baronesa* for more than one voyage that the ship was jinxed could be said to be justified. Few months passed by when her name did not appear in the casualty column of 'Lloyd's Lists'. Groundings, fires in her bunkers, collisions, machinery breakdowns - all soon became commonplace. During the Second World War it was said that U-boat captains had instructions never to sink her but only harass, as she was more nuisance to the British afloat than she would be if sent to the bottom! In this brief account of Furness-Houlder Argentine Line ships, space does not allow for more than a mention of three of the ship's more serious misfortunes; one just three months before the outbreak of the Second World War, and a couple during hostilities.

At the beginning of June 1939, the national newspapers and wireless broadcasts were full of the tragedy of HMS *Thetis*, a new submarine which, whilst on trials on the first of the month, sank with heavy loss

of life. Not surprising therefore, that a boiler explosion on board a British cargo ship exactly one month later, though responsible for four deaths, received no publicity other than its inclusion in 'Lloyd's List's' casualty column. The *Baronesa*, which had recently undergone a survey and dry docking, was fully laden in Liverpool docks and preparing for sea when the explosion occurred on 1st July 1939, its force killing the engineer on watch and two fireman, a third subsequently dying in hospital.

September 1940 saw the massive attack by waves of enemy aircraft on London Docks in which many ships were seriously damaged and others sunk where they lay. On the 7th September around 6.00 pm a high-explosive bomb landed on the edge of the dockside at numbers 25/27 sheds, Royal Albert Dock, abreast the *Baronesa's* number 4 hold, the force of the explosion blowing a large hole in the side of the ship. She was fully laden with meat, and awaiting the departure of the *Duquesa* from Z Shed, Royal Victoria Docks in order to take her place and discharge her cargo. She immediately commenced to take water in number 4 hold, which rose to a height of seven feet above the orlop deck, spreading to number 5 hold where it reached 3 feet 6 inches, whilst in the engine room water flooded to a height of 11 feet. The ship took on a list to starboard until she all but leaned against the dockside whilst at the same time settling on the bottom of the dock. Forward areas of the vessel were isolated by the closing of watertight doors,

Working continuously from the 7th to 11th September, the ship's pumps gradually gained some control and from the 12th an Admiralty salvage officer took charge, providing a diver and salvage crew, the former making a full examination of the hull and the latter plugging where necessary. Continued pumping gradually reduced the list but it was not until the 24th that the ship was sufficiently upright for numbers 4 and 5 holds to be opened up and its - by now - stinking cargo discharged overside into barges for towing down river to the soap factories at Queenborough on the Isle of Sheppey, the work being carried out by a special, fully masked decontamination squad. Throughout this period the area continued to be the Luftwaffe's 'target for tonight' with periodic daylight raids thrown in. From personal experience of this episode, the writer can vouch for the discomfort of living aboard a vessel with its decks equivalent to a mountainside, and the extinguishing of incendiary bombs a nightly pastime. Mercifully no further high-explosive bombs landed close enough to interrupt work in progress.

The *Baronesa*'s wartime misfortune which had the most bizarre outcome began on 13th September 1942, when she was lying at the deep water berth at South Dock, Buenos Aires. Fire broke out in her bunkers and rapidly spread, causing considerable damage, and only when the weight of water poured upon her caused her to submerge and rest on the dock bottom was it finally extinguished. With only her masts and funnel above water, it was nine days before she was raised when, but for the shortage of refrigerated ships, she would almost certainly have been sold to ship breakers. Every part of her was covered in thick, clinging, foul-smelling slime. Her crew, meanwhile - most of whom had lost all their possessions and left with only the clothes they stood up in - had been accommodated in the International Hotel ashore. On their return they faced a formidable task. Every inch of the ship had to be cleaned and, as an engineer later described it to the writer, down in the engine room this first seemed nigh on impossible and was the most heart- and back-breaking job a man could encounter. Similarly, only sheer determination and dedication finally resulted in the insulated holds, with their miles of piping lining both deckheads and bulkheads, being restored to a cleanliness essential for the loading of meat.

Three months later, when order had been restored, temporary repairs effected and the *Baronesa* declared seaworthy, she loaded a full cargo. Leaving Buenos Aires on 31st December she arrived at Montevideo on New Year's Day 1943, where some holes

were found in her lifeboats which had to be repaired before she could proceed.

In the short passage between the Argentine and Uruguayan capitals it had become obvious that the ship's engines could only produce a slow speed. Accordingly, the ship's master, Captain G.N. Brien, warned of heavy U-boat activity, was not prepared to risk the unescorted crossing to Freetown, where a convoy would have been joined, and decided on a southbound passage via the Straits of Magellenes.

With the Straits safely negotiated and now heading northwards, the ship had reached a point about three days sailing from Panama when a US cruiser hove in sight, and refusing to believe the *Baronesa* was a British merchantman, sent a boarding party across, which accused Captain Brien of being a German who had mastered the English language. Suspicion had been aroused by the cross on the ship's funnel which, though painted out, could still be seen. (The 1918 ships and later the *Hardwicke Grange* of 1921 bore a cross of metal separate from the main structure of the funnel, and made fast to it with struts). The cruiser, joined by a destroyer, then escorted their prize to Colon, reached on 25th January 1943. By 3rd February the Americans had, however, accepted the true identity of the ship, but in the meantime the British Admiralty had jumped to an unfortunate conclusion. On about this date Houlder Brothers received a message to the effect that, as nothing had been heard of the *Baronesa* for a considerable time, it must be concluded that the vessel had been lost. This information was never corrected and so no blame could be attached to the company, in ignorance of the true situation, for relaying the false information to the next of kin of the ship's entire company.

Having transited the Panama Canal, the *Baronesa* anchored in Guantanamo Bay, Cuba at 12.30 am on 7th February, proceeding at 8.00 am the following morning. Arrived off New York in a temperature of 30 degrees below, and condensing steam in her pipes frozen solid, it took 20 minutes to drop anchor, and three days to raise it again before moving in to berth at a pier next to the burnt-out *Normandie*.

Three weeks later the ship sailed for Halifax, again escorted by US warships, and there followed an ice-breaker into the inner harbour. Leaks having been found just below the waterline and in the forepeak area, temporary repairs were made with cement boxes, and on the 20th February she sailed from Halifax, in convoy, arriving at Liverpool on the 2nd April 1943.

Unlike the *Duquesa*, and despite all, the *Baronesa* survived the war but was the first of the remaining three 1918 ships to make her way to shipbreakers. This followed arrival at London at the end of her last voyage on 17th August 1946, when she remained laid up for the next four months. *Princesa* and *Marquesa* continued in service until 1949.

Duquesa seen above, arriving in Liverpool, and right when flying the German flag following her capture by the *Admiral von Scheer*. [B. & A. Feilden, D.H. Johnzon collection; D.H. Johnzon collection]

The loss of the *Duquesa* has featured in many books so that little more that a passing reference is needed here.

Sailing from Rio de Janeiro watched by those aboard *El Argentino* on 6th December 1940, *Duquesa* was captured by the German pocket battleship *Admiral von Scheer*, and with a prize crew on board taken south to a German rendezvous known as Andalucia. There, with her cargo of 5,000 tons of meat and 14.5 million eggs, she was obliged to act as a supply ship to armed merchant raiders and submarines alike. Andalucia, however, covered many square miles. Steam had to be kept up both for periodic movement and to maintain the refrigeration, but the Germans were determined that she should remain afloat until every last ounce of her goodies had been transferred, late arrivals leading to considerable delay. In due course the ship's bunkers were exhausted but, not to be denied, every wooden item on board which could be removed, from wheelhouse and chart room to wood-caulked decking was fed into the ship's furnaces. Only when the last hint of meat and the final egg had found its way to German mouths was the vessel declared redundant. Explosive charges were placed in her engine room and the renamed *Herzogin* (German for duchess, or duquesa) sent to the bottom on 18th February 1941, two months to the day after her capture. Crew and passengers, meanwhile, had been placed on board three prison ships to be taken to Germany via Bordeaux and there to remain for the duration of the war.

Post-war acquisitions

Intended as replacements for meat carrying ships lost in the First World War, one through enemy action, contracts were signed on behalf of the Shipping Controller with four shipyards for a total of 29 ships capable of a speed of 13 to 14 knots. As only one was completed before hostilities ceased, however, seven were cancelled and the majority completed for private ownership. Known as type 'G', they fell into two categories, 14 being built as twin-screw steamers with reciprocating machinery and the remaining eight with a single screw and turbine driven. Of these, only one was laid down with a 'War' name and purchased whilst under construction. 'War' names had been reserved for the remaining seven, but were not required for the vessels being acquired by private owners prior to keel laying. Furness-Houlder Argentine Line were the buyers of the penultimate construction, Workman Clark and Co.'s yard number 449, completed in November 1920 as the company's second *Canonesa*, by which name she had been laid down. That she might have been built as *War Minerva*, as recorded elsewhere, is guesswork.

Of the 'G' type ships, *Canonesa* had the largest space for refrigerated cargoes. She gave excellent service and it was most unfortunate that during the Second World War she was the first of the type to be sunk, a victim of U 100 during a concentrated attack upon convoy HX72 in which 12 ships were lost. She was under the command of Captain F. Stephenson. One life was lost, that of the fourth engineer, Tom Purnell, on watch in the engine room at the time the torpedo struck.

In 1928 the British and Argentine Steam Navigation Co. Ltd. acquired its last ship. She was the motor vessel *El Argentino* - second of that name - identical twin sister of Houlder Line's *Dunster Grange*, the two ships built alongside one another at the Glasgow yard of Fairfield Shipbuilding and Engineering Co. Ltd. with the Houlder Line vessel completed in January and the *El Argentino* in April.

Mention was made earlier of Manchester Liner's determination to retain an interest in the South American meat trade, first obtained through the charter of the company's 1898-built steamer *Manchester City* to the Anglo-Argentine Shipping Co. in 1906 and continued on completion of that charter by separate contracts with meat companies in Argentina and elsewhere. In 1928 the 30-year-old steamer was sold to Norwegian shipbreakers and, to continue its association with South America, Manchester Liners bought a 50% interest in the new *El Argentino*, retaining it for the lifetime of the vessel. Despite this be it noted, no entry has been found on Lloyd's Voyage Record Cards for this ship (the data thereon extracted from the ship movements columns of 'Lloyd's List') of any visit to the port of Manchester, her discharge ports in the U.K. appearing as London in the main and occasionally Liverpool, at least until 1940 when Belfast, Swansea and Cardiff began to appear.

El Argentino and *Dunster Grange*, 15.5-knot ships, twin-screw and propelled by Fairfield-Sulzer oil engines and of 9,501 and 9,494 gross tons respectively, vied for the position of largest meat carriers of their day, but there was very little in it; with the *El Argentino* just having the edge with 557,500 cubic feet of refrigerated space against the *Dunster Grange's* 556,840 cubic feet. Both set new high standards of excellence in all departments and their passenger accommodation for 12 in single-berth cabins would have put many a full-blown passenger liner to shame.

The winding up of the British and Argentine Steam Navigation Co. on 16th August 1933, and transfer of its three remaining ships to Furness-Houlder Argentine Lines could have been seen as no more than a paper transaction, since the River Plate liner service, with all ships in Houlder colours, crewed with Houlder sea staffs, continued to operate as hitherto. *El Uruguayo* and *La Rosarina*, however, were sold to shipbreakers in 1937 having just been preceded by Houlder Line's *El Paraguayo*.

Canonesa in the Mersey. *Canonesa* was built to the standard First World War G design; one of several sold to private owners before the keel was laid. 'War' names had been reserved for use if no buyers were found, but none were required.
[B. & A. Feilden, D.H. Johnzon collection]

The *El Argentino's* days came to a sad end during the Second World War when she was bombed off Portugal, in position 39.50 north by 13.38 west, whilst in convoy OS52KM on a voyage from Glasgow to Buenos Aires in ballast. She was under the command of Captain F.W. Kent, who later became Houlder's Commodore Captain of the Line. The date was 26th July 1943, but she was believed to have had a narrow escape much earlier, in December 1940, when VIPs amongst her passengers may well have saved her.

When dealing with the capture of the *Duquesa*, mention was made of members of the *El Argentino's* crew watching her sail from Rio de Janeiro on 6th December 1940. The *El Argentino* had put into Rio, but not to top up with fruit or eggs, but more as a precaution. Her passengers had come aboard at Montevideo and probably chief among them was the 16 year-old daughter of the British Ambassador to Uruguay. Jean Millington-Drake, who was also the granddaughter of Lord Inchcape, homeward bound to stay with relations in Cornwall. The young lass had a companion not very much older than herself. Just one other lady passenger was the wife of the overseer at a Shell Refinery in Argentina. Among the male passengers was a certain French officer - Colonel Petit - of some importance in Free French circles, whose safe arrival was said to be eagerly awaited by General de Gaulle. Additionally there was an archbishop of the Catholic Church. Neither of these two gents was too proud to keep a watch on deck, seeking telltale signs of submarines.

Several hours after the departure of the *Duquesa*, the *El Argentino* also sailed, but on a northerly passage, hugging the coast of Brazil, then cutting across to refuel at St. Vincent, Cape Verde Islands, arriving on 19th December 1940 and departing the same day. Crossing the notorious Bay of Biscay she encountered not only the worst weather of the voyage but of her career, according to the chippy who had served in her since she was built. Despite this no serious damage was done and being 25th December all the good fare of Christmas was served for those capable of tackling it.

In contrast there followed six days of thick fog but the genius of a navigating officer enabled Inisfallen Light to be picked up as the fog lifted, within one hour of estimated time.

El Argentino arrived in the Clyde on New Year's Eve, too late unfortunately to obtain clearance for shore going. Determined that his passengers should not be entirely deprived of the joy of welcoming in the New Year, Captain Henry Heal decided to hold a dance in the saloon. Needless to say there was a certain imbalance as between males and females in attendance. Just three ladies were obliged to cope with the attentions of master and four deck officers, chief engineer and four or five others from his department, three radio officers, the ship's doctor and five eager young deck apprentices. In desperation, Captain Heal summoned the stewardess, about to enjoy an early night

prior to leaving the ship to conform with the company's instructions that, for the duration of the war, stewardesses would not be employed aboard Houlder-managed ships. To her credit she made the effort, though the addition of one lady hardly made any great difference. Captain Heal at least had done his best and amidst much laughter and cheering 1941 came on board.
To be continued

El Argentino, sailing from Liverpool. Attached to this photo is a note from Dennis: 'On the bridge it was impossible to hear yourself think, never mind the instructions from Captain Henry Heal who, having lost the roof of his mouth, spoke from the top of his nose. The so-called noise eliminator on the after end on the bridge seemed to work in reverse. For her twin sister, *Dunster Grange*, her engineers has a very suitable name - *Dustbin Grange*.' [B.& A.Feilden, D.H.Johnzon collection]

Fleet list part 2

12. BARONESA 1918-1946
O.N. 140583 Call signs: JTQK/GPDS 8,663g 5,408n 431.0 x 61.3 x 38.6 (F: 39 feet; B: 259 feet).
Two T. 3-cyl. by Richardsons, Westgarth and Co. Ltd., Middlesbrough driving twin screws (Engine No. 2244); each 25½, 41½, 70 x 48 inches; 14½ knots
1929: Cylinders recorded as port: 25½, 42¼, 70 x 48 inches; starboard: 25½, 42, 70 x 48 inches.
12 first class passengers.
Refrigeration equipment: two engines plus two compressors, carbon dioxide/brine/silicate cotton with 'Ozonaire' facilities for carriage of oranges by J. and E. Hall Ltd., Dartford, Kent; 467,001 cubic feet in 46 chambers; 475,000 cubic feet in 43 chambers.
4.1918: Completed by Sir Raylton Dixon and Co. Ltd., Middlesbrough (Yard No. 593) for Furness-Houlder

Argentine Lines Ltd. (Houlder Brothers and Co. Ltd., manager), Liverpool as BARONESA.
Maiden voyage: Captain H.P. Goodricks.
6.8.1938: Whilst lying at anchor in Holyhead Bay in fog run down by passenger steamer HIBERNIA (3,467/1920 London, Midland and Scottish Railway, London) at 4.00 am with damage to both vessels. HIBERNIA held to blame at subsequent enquiry.
1.7.1939: Boiler explosion killed four men when preparing to depart from Liverpool.
7.9.1940: Seriously damaged by high explosive bomb which exploded on the dockside at Number 25/27 Sheds, Royal Albert Dock, London, when waiting to discharge 5,000 tons of meat. Water affected cargo in numbers 4 and 5 holds and flooded engine room. Affected meat sold to soap factories at Queenborough, Isle of Sheppey after ship pumped out and righted. Repairs implemented but

vessel out of commission for several months.
3.5.1941: Whilst at anchor in River Mersey awaiting departure sustained further bomb damage when a high explosive bomb exploded underwater close by stern causing water to enter through buckled after-peak tank bulkhead and via after tunnel well. Returned to dock for repairs and eventually sailed on 16.5.1941.
13.9.1942: Seriously damaged when fire broke out in her bunkers and rapidly spread whilst lying at South Dock, Buenos Aires. Entire crew obliged to abandon vessel, many losing all their possessions, when submerged to dock bottom.
31.12.1942: Sailed, having been temporarily repaired and thoroughly cleaned after raising and ultimately loading a full cargo. With engines unable to cope with more than a few knots, it was decided to make the homeward passage via the Straits of

Magellenes, during the course of which the ship was arrested by a US Navy cruiser on suspicion of being an enemy vessel. She had been reported by the Admiralty as presumed lost. Escorted through the Panama Canal to New York and eventually to Halifax for further repairs and a convoy home, reaching Liverpool 2.4.1943.

The above represents just a very few of the series of casualties with which the BARONESA was afflicted for the greater part of her career.

3.12.1946: Sold to Belgian shipbreakers.

6.12.1946: Arrived Burcht and later dismantled at Sas van Ghent.

Total service: 28½ years.

13. DUQUESA (1) 1918-1940

O.N. 140578 Call sign: JTMG/GPDT
8,651g 5,400n 429.6 x 61.3 x 38.6 feet (F: 37 feet, B: 257 feet).
12 first class passengers.
Two T. 3-cyl. by Richardsons, Westgarth and Co. Ltd., Hartlepool driving twin screws (Engine No. 2333 H); each 25, 41½, 70 x 48 inches; 14½ knots.
Refrigeration equipment: two engines plus two compressors, carbon dioxide/brine/silicate cotton by J. and E. Hall Ltd., Dartford, Kent; 464,838 cubic feet in 46 chambers, 470,157 cubic feet in 41 chambers.
Number 1 shelter, orlop and lower hold decks fitted with 'Ozonaire' for carriage of oranges. Number 4 bridge trunk, shelter hold and trunk fitted for the carriage of bananas. Other fruit facilities in number 6 shelter and main deck spaces.

5.1918: Completed by Irvine's Shipbuilding and Engineering Co. Ltd., West Hartlepool (Yard No. 555) for Furness-Houlder Argentine Lines Ltd. (Houlder Brothers and Co. Ltd.,

managers), Liverpool as DUQUESA. Maiden voyage: Captain G. Jarvis.

5.1940: Whilst discharging meat at Le Havre the docks were bombed by enemy aircraft. The DUQUESA was one of the last Allied ships to leave the port before the enemy invaded the area.

18.12.1940: Captured by German battleship ADMIRAL SCHEER in position 00.57 north by 22.42 west when homeward bound from River Plate and Rio de Janeiro for Freetown and the Clyde with a cargo of 5,000 tons of meat and 14½ million eggs. The master, Captain L. Bearpark, the first and second radio officers, gunnery officer and one apprentice taken aboard the raider. Prize crew boarded the DUQUESA which, given the name HERZOGIN (German for Duquesa), was sailed southwards to a rendezvous of German ships and submarines known as Andalucia. There she was used as a supply ship, her entire cargo and stores being transferred to German vessels over the next two months.

17.2.1941: Last of the ship's crew and her few passengers taken off and put aboard prison ships, in which they were taken to Bordeaux and thence to German prison camps for the duration of the war.

18.2.1941: Explosive charges placed in ship's engine room, ship sinking upon detonation.

Total service: 22½ years.

14. PRINCESA 1918-1949

O.N. 140585 Call sign: PTSC/GPDW
8,731g 5,433n 430.2 x 61.2 x 36.0 feet (F: 35 feet, B 255 feet).
12 first class passengers.
Two T. 3-cyl. by Alexander Stephen and Sons Ltd., Govan, Glasgow

(Engine No. 467); each 25, 41½, 70 x 48 inches; 14½ knots.
Refrigeration equipment: two engines plus two compressors, carbon dioxide/brine/cork by J. and E. Hall Ltd., Dartford, Kent; 454,834 cubic feet in 48 chambers, 472,500 cubic feet in 45 chambers.
Provision for carriage of fruit, bananas and other fruit as BARONESA and DUQUESA above.

7.1918: Completed by Alexander Stephen and Sons Ltd., Govan, Glasgow (Yard No. 467) for Furness-Houlder Argentine Lines Ltd. (Houlder Brothers and Co. Ltd., managers), Liverpool as PRINCESA. Maiden voyage: Captain W.R. Coleman.

24.7.1926: Reported in the *Times* to have lost starboard propeller when about 250 miles off the Cape Verde Isles, on a homeward voyage with meat from Buenos Aires and Montevideo. No damage had been sustained and she was prodeeding at eight knots and had plenty of fuel. No assistance was required.

12.5.1940: Sailed from Montevideo with a special cargo consigned to the Admiralty, which had been delivered to the ship by private contractor the previous day. It comprised a 4.1 inch twin gun salvaged from the wreck of the German battleship GRAF SPEE; to

Princesa was the author's favourite ship. He always said that after the vibration and noise of *El Argentino's (2)* machinery the silence above decks on *Princesa* was sheer heaven, despite coal dust in the ears, nose and throat and even in one's bunk after refuelling. *[D.H.Johnzon collection]*

Marquesa is seen first, top, as completed in July 1918, dazzle painted, and without topmasts. She has a single tall moveable radio mast amidships. Its position was intended to disguise the direction in which the ship was heading. *[D.H. Johnzon collection]*

The middle photograph shows *Marquesa* in peacetime colours off Cape Town. *Marquesa* differed from her consorts in having only a token boat deck, comprising a platform aft on which stood the radio room and accommodation for second and third radio officers and apprentices, with forward of this a narrow catwalk on either side of the engine room skylight. Her four life-boats were housed at bridge level. A copy of the Board of Trade Passenger Certificate in the author's possession, dated 1st August 1918, licenses her for 16 first class passengers and 104 crew. In view of her lack of a proper boat deck, it was difficult to meet the

certificate's provision that 'all passengers are to have sufficient promenade space on deck'.*[Ships in Focus, D.H. Johnzon collection]*

The bottom photograph shows *Marquesa* during her second war. *[D.H. Johnzon collection]*

take the weight of which the PRINCESA's foredeck had earlier been strengthened under the supervision of Captain H. Daniel, Houlder's Marine Superintendent at Montevideo. More importantly, however, the consignment contained radar equipment which had provided the GRAF SPEE with such accurate fire and had been brought up from the wreck by divers directed by Royal Navy experts who had arrived in Montevideo posing as employees of T.W. Ward Ltd. intent on disposing of the wreck to overcome the navigational hazard for ships entering or leaving the port. On board PRINCESA this material was stowed below decks. At Freetown she joined Convoy SL 34 which sailed for the U.K. on 31.5.1940. It was attacked by U-boats on 12th June and two ships, BARBARA MARIE (4,223/1928; Cliffside Shipping Co. Ltd., J. Morrison and Son, Newcastle-upon-Tyne) and WILLOWBANK (3,041/1939, Bank Line Ltd., Andrew Weir and Co., London), were sunk, the former with a cargo of iron ore with heavy loss of life. The suggestion that the German's had been determined to sink the PRINCESA and prevent her cargo reaching British experts' hands, but had sunk the wrong ship, was later discounted. On 16th June she is reported to have made a call at Plymouth, before completing her voyage at Liverpool on 18th June.
23.6.1949: Sold to Hughes Bolckow Shipbreakers Co. for £23,000
12.7.1949: Left Liverpool in tow for Blyth.
Total service: 31 years.

15. MARQUESA 1918-1949
O.N. 140586 Call signs: JTSN/GPDY 8,979g 5,604n 430.2 x 61.1 x 35.7 feet (F: 41 feet; B: 257 feet).
Two T. 3-cyl. by David Rowan and Co. Ltd., Glasgow driving twin screws (Engine Nos. 642/3);each 26, 42½/70 x 45 inches; 14½ knots.
12 first class passengers.
Refrigeration equipment: two engines plus two compressors, Carbon dioxide/brine/silicate cotton by J. and E. Hall Ltd., Dartford, Kent; 433,000 cubic feet in 43 chambers. 457,493 cubic feet in 48 chambers.
7.1918: Completed by William Hamilton and Co. Ltd., Port Glasgow (Yard No. 303) for Furness-Houlder Argentine Lines Ltd. (Houlder Brothers and Co. Ltd., managers), Liverpool as MARQUESA.
22.5.1923: Reported in the *Times* to have stranded at Las Palmas, lying on a hard bottom abaft number 4 hold but afloat forward, leaking badly aft, with propeller blades bent and one blade of port propeller broken.
24.5.1923: Reported refloated without assistance and moored alongside quay.

26.5.1943: Minor damage when grounded in River Plate whilst on passage from Buenos Aires to Montevideo.
15.11.1943: Fouled wreck of the motor vessel INNISFALLEN (3,071/1930, British and Irish Steam Packet Co Ltd., Dublin) in the River Mersey. Towed off but leaks developed necessitating discharge of cargo just loaded at Liverpool in numbers 1 and 2 holds. Temporary plates fitted whilst vessel pumped dry.
11.12.1943: Reloaded and sailed.
19.7.1944: Ashore at Cape St. Vincent, Second Narrows, Straits of Magellan. Damaged and leaking in numbers 1, 2 and 3 holds, with 10 feet of water in number 2. Captain of port of Punta Arenas arrived in steamer AUSTRAL and naval tug awaited instructions. Ship found to be aground along whole length except 24 feet from bows. Lower holds forward tidal. 1,200 tons meat discharged, with sound meat taken to freezer at Rio Seco, damaged meat sold to Tres Puentas Tallow Co. Salvage of vessel on no cure-no pay basis undertaken.
26.7.1944: Refloated. Temporary repairs agreed at £5,500.
17.8.1944: Following extensive repairs, undamaged cargo re-shipped at Rio Seco.
9.10.1945: At Halifax with boiler trouble, a later report advising that all boilers were in poor condition, dirty and in need of repairs.
23.10.1945: Dry-docked, with crew unable to close injection valves, condenser leaking, five boilers badly salted, and other repairs needed.
28.10.1945: Repairs completed and sailed.
29.10.1948: Arrived at Liverpool on completion of final voyage. Laid up to await sale.
1.3.1949: Sold to BISCO for £23,000 and allocated to T.W. Ward Ltd.
14.3.1949: Arrived at Barrow-in-Furness under tow.
Total service: 30½ years.

16. CANONESA (2) 1920-1940
O.N. 143660 Call sign: GCKM 8,286g 5,102n 450.0 x 58.4 x 40.0 feet (F: 44 feet; P: 35 feet).
Two double-reduction geared turbines driving a single-screw shaft by Workman, Clark and Co. Ltd., Belfast (Engine No. 449); 14 knots.
Refrigeration equipment: two single engines, carbon dioxide/brine/cork and silicate cotton by J. and E. Hall Ltd., Dartford, Kent; 456,576 cubic feet in 18 chambers.
11.1920: Completed by Workman, Clark and Co. Ltd., Belfast (Yard No. 449) for Furness-Houlder Argentine Lines Ltd. (Houlder Brothers and Co. Ltd., managers), Liverpool as CANONESA.
4.4.1940: Sailed from London on penultimate voyage, number 53 (see text).

21.9.1940: Torpedoed and sunk by the German submarine U 100 in position 54.55 north by 18.26 west whilst on a voyage from Montreal to Liverpool via Sydney, Cape Breton, in Convoy HX 72 with 7,265 tons of refrigerated cargo, including 2,258 tons of bacon, 995 tons of cheese, 250 tons of ham, 379 tons of fish plus frozen and chilled beef. One man, the fouth engineer, was lost from her complement of 62 crew and one gunner. She was under the command of Captain F.Stephenson.
Total service: 20½ years.

17. ELARGENTINO 1928-1943
O.N. 160405 Call sign: GNQD 9,501g 6,023n 431.3 x 64.5 x 35.4 feet (F: 82 feet; B: 250 feet)
12 first class passengers
Two Fairfield-Sulzer 6-cyl. 2SCSA oil engines by the Fairfield Shipbuilding and Engineering Co. Ltd., Govan driving twin screws; 1,710 NHP, 6,400 BHP, 14½ knots.
Refrigeration equipment: two units and four compressors, carbon dioxide/brine and air by J. and E. Hall Ltd., Dartford, Kent 557,500 cubic feet in 53 chambers. 558,360 cubic feet in 53 chambers.
11.1.1928: Launched by the Fairfield Shipbuilding and Engineering Co. Ltd., Govan (Yard No. 629).
4.1928: Completed.
5.4.1928: Registered in the ownership of the British and Argentine Steam Navigation Co. Ltd. and Manchester Liners Ltd., Manchester (Houlder Brothers and Co. Ltd., London, managers) as EL ARGENTINO.
24.1.1934: Owners became Furness, Withy and Co. Ltd., London.
10.3.1941: A message from Buenos Aires reported engine damage during heavy weather when outward bound.
7.1.1942: A grounding in the estuary at Montevideo led to further engine troubles. From Halifax a message was received advising engines in urgent need of repair.
19.6.1942: Arrived Freetown from Montevideo with serious engine trouble. Remained until 26.8.1942 during which time some repairs were undertaken.
26.7.1943: Bombed and sunk by German aircraft north west of Lisbon in position 39.50 north by 13.36 west whilst in convoy OS 52/KMS 21 on a voyage from Glasgow to Montevideo and Buenos Aires in ballast. Struck by bombs from a Focke-Wulf Condor flying at 17,000 feet and out of range of escort's fire, she sank in 30 minutes. Four of the 88 on board were lost. The tug EMPIRE SAMSON picked up some survivors, later transferring them to the corvette HMS JONQUIL, which in turn transferred them to HMS MALLOW.
23.12.1943: Register closed.
Total service: 15 years.

THE LAST YEARS OF THE LOCH LINE – Part 1
Malcolm Cooper

By the start of the twentieth century, the Glasgow ship-owners Aitken, Lilburn and Co. had been operating their Loch Line sailing ship service between the UK and Australia for 30 years. In retrospect, the day of the sailing ship had passed in the closing decades of the previous century but, at the time, there were still some 1,000 large deep-water sailing vessels on the UK register. Although new vessel construction had all but ended in the UK after a last wave of investment in the early 1890s, there were still a large number of UK ship-owners who remained wedded to sail and showed no sign of transferring to the steamships that had already driven their vessels from all but the long-distance bulk trades. What was unusual about Aitken, Lilburn and Co. was that they were not really operating in the long-distance tramp trades like most other owners. Rather they were still running their business around its initial concept, as a liner service on a fixed route: outwards from Glasgow with general cargo and passengers for Adelaide and Melbourne, and then from the latter port homewards to London, normally with wool.

A mixture of technological advances and changing trade conditions had been undermining the fundamentals of the business for some time. The last purpose-built wool clippers, Donaldson Rose's *Cromdale* and *Mount Stewart*, had been built in 1891, and the most famous wool clipper of all, the *Cutty Sark*, had made her last voyage under the red ensign in 1895. In order to remain competitive in the face of the steam-ship, sailing ship building had moved away from an emphasis on speed to an emphasis on economical carrying capacity, replacing fine-lined clippers with large sail plans with broad-hulled carriers rigged to minimize crew requirements. Sail was still a viable option to carry wool and grain from Australia to Europe, but the remnants of the once grand wool fleet had to compete

A splendid line up of Loch Line vessels in Victoria Dock, Melbourne over Christmas 1907. From the left, *Loch Etive, Loch Broom, Loch Garry, Loch Katrine, Loch Carron* with *Loch Tay* alongside and *Loch Torridon. [Port of Melbourne Authority, Author's collection]*

The Loch Line service ended with the arrival in the Channel in 1911 of the 1881-built iron barque *Loch Torridon*. She is seen at Port Adelaide in 1905. *[John Naylon collection]*

not only with an increasing number of steam vessels on both liner and tramp services, but also with sail general traders driven out of other trades by these same steamers. Perhaps more seriously, the outward general cargo and passenger trade from the UK had contracted to a level where sailing ships were unlikely to make a profit. Australian industrialization had reduced the demand for many manufactured goods, and much of the remainder went by steam. After 1900, drought and rabbit plague in Australia put further downwards pressure on ocean freight rates. On the passenger side, only an adventurous minority of migrants were likely to choose a sailing ship berth over a safer and more comfortable one in a passenger liner offering a far more predictable voyage time.

In the face of all this, the Loch Line soldiered on until 1911, the service finally coming to an end when the *Loch Broom* and the *Loch Torridon* arrived in London within five days of each other in May of that year. The last decade, however, had been a painful experience of misfortune and almost constant financial loss. In retrospect, it seems incredible that the company did not see the writing on the wall and sell up far earlier.

Aitken, Lilburn and Co. had begun the Loch Line service in 1869-70 when they formed the Glasgow Shipping Co. and ordered six 1,250-ton iron sailing vessels from two Clyde shipbuilders. James Aitken and James Lilburn were the managers rather than the owners of the vessels themselves, whose construction was actually financed by a consortium of Glasgow businessmen. In 1873, a second company, the General Shipping Co., was formed, this time with a slightly different group of investors, but again managed by Aitken and Lilburn. Originally the Glasgow Shipping Co. was intended to serve Melbourne and

the General Shipping Co. Sydney, but over time the two businesses were merged in operational terms and only retained their separate identities for shareholding purposes. Neither company ever sought limited liability status, and as death or business failure reduced the ranks of the original shareholders the survivors took over the shares of those who had left with Aitken and Lilburn themselves becoming increasingly important shareholders in the 1870s.

The Loch Line operated a total of 24 vessels (22 built to its order and two acquired second-hand) of which 19 were acquired in the first decade of the line's existence. The first 19 vessels were all iron three-masters of 1,250 to 1,600 tons built for speed. Good-sized vessels for their day, they were small by the standards of the end of the century, with their carrying capacity reduced by their fine lines. In the early 1880s, the line added two pairs of 2,000 ton four-masters. Finally, almost a decade after the last of these entered service, the firm ordered one larger four-masted barque, built along the far fuller lines typical of the last generation of commercial sailing ships. Losses to this fleet were heavy. Between 1871, when the *Loch Leven* was wrecked in the Bass Strait at the start of a homeward voyage and 1899, when the *Loch Sloy* was wrecked off Adelaide at the end of an outward one, a total of 10 ships were lost. Three of these went missing, three each were wrecked in Australian and European waters, and one was lost in collision. The fleet was further reduced in 1900 when its most recent addition, the 2,400 ton *Loch Nevis*, was sold after only six years service, having failed to establish herself on the regular service. The departure of the *Loch Nevis* reduced the fleet to 13 vessels, of which five were over 30 years old and only three had been built after 1880. The general pattern of the service was to load general cargo at Glasgow and sail outwards to Adelaide. The vessels then sailed on to Melbourne from where they generally sailed homewards for London, either with wool or grain (although the home destination was sometimes varied in line with the requirements of charters). A round voyage normally took approximately a year, although only a little over half this time would be spent at sea.

Maritime losses

The Loch Line's ageing fleet suffered a series of further misfortunes in the early years of the new century. In November 1901, the *Loch Vennachar* was run down and sunk in shallow water by the Wilson steamer *Cato* (924/1867) while at anchor off Thameshaven waiting to proceed upstream to unload her cargo of wool at London. The vessel was 26 years old at the time, but she was one of the fastest ships in the fleet and her owners were sufficiently committed to the future to have her raised and towed to Tilbury for repairs.

There was no hope of reprieve for the line's next maritime casualty. The *Loch Long* was among the first ships in the fleet to be reduced to barque rig, and perhaps because of a poor speed record was deployed away from the normal homeward voyage pattern. On 29th April 1903 she sailed from New Caledonia with a cargo of nickel ore for Glasgow with a crew of 24. She never arrived. Wreckage washed up on the Chatham Islands suggested that she had not proceeded far on her voyage before being wrecked or overwhelmed by the elements.

The next serious incident occurred a year and

a half later at the other end of the world. The *Loch Carron* was three days out from Glasgow, some 80 miles south west of Fastnet when she ran down the Greenock barque *Inverkip*. The *Inverkip*, which was inward bound from Melbourne to Queenstown with a cargo of grain, sank immediately and only two men who managed to jump onto the *Loch Carron* at the moment of impact survived. The *Loch Carron's* collision bulkhead held and she was able to limp into Queenstown for repairs, but she was found to blame for the collision and her owners and insurers had to bear the full cost of the loss of *Inverkip* and her cargo. In one of the dreadful coincidences that so often seem to attend such tragedies, Captain Stainton Clarke of the *Loch Carron* was a personal friend of Captain Jones of the *Inverkip*, who was lost with his wife in the sinking. Clarke was so badly affected by the incident that he had to be relieved of his command before the repaired *Loch Carron* sailed again. This was to be the only occasion on which the ship would sail under the red ensign without Clarke in command. He had taken her from her builders in 1885, commanded her on her first 17 voyages to the southern hemisphere, and would return after the one voyage interruption to command her until her sale in 1912.

The following year witnessed the company's last marine casualty. The *Loch Vennachar* enjoyed only a brief reprieve after her rescue from the bottom of the Thames. On 6th September 1905 she was spoken by a local trading vessel 160 miles west of Neptune Island, 84 days out of Glasgow and only a few days away from her destination Adelaide. She never arrived, and although eventually posted missing at Lloyd's, the discovery of wreckage along the rugged coast of Kangaroo Island suggested that she had met

Seen at Melbourne, the iron ship *Loch Vennachar* of 1875 was sunk in the Thames in 1901, but raised and returned to service, despite her age. She disappeared in 1905. *[John Naylon collection]*

the same fate as her fleet mate the *Loch Sloy*, wrecked there only six years before. Her fate was finally confirmed almost 70 years later in 1976 when divers found her wreck jammed at the bottom of a huge fissure in 100-foot cliffs. The loss of both vessels echoed the much more celebrated loss of the *Loch Ard* in the earlier years of the service. Approaching Australia on the Great Circle route, a sailing ship master had no prior landfalls to guide him. Even a small error in navigation could prove fatal in avoiding the high cliffs of Kangaroo Island and the coast around Cape Otway, particularly at night.

Above: *Loch Carron* at Cape Town. Apart from one voyage, Captain Stainton Clarke was in command from her completion in 1885 until her sale to Norwegian owners 27 years later. *[Solomon, John Naylon collection]*

Right: *Loch Sloy* of 1877, rigged as a barque at Melbourne. Note that her jibboom is housed to save berthing space. *Loch Sloy* was wrecked on Kangaroo Island in April 1899 with the loss of all but three of her complement. *[John Naylon collection]*

Trading losses

This sorry list of disasters was made all the worse by the fact that the Loch Line was suffering an almost unrelieved series of unprofitable voyage results. The collection of surviving voyage records is incomplete, but those for almost every voyage undertaken from 1903 survive in the Mitchell Library in Glasgow. Of the 60 voyages whose results are thus preserved, only 20 produced a profit, and in only six of the latter was the profit more than £500. Taking the voyages together, the line recorded a loss in every year between 1904 and 1911. Looking at the results on an average vessel-by-vessel basis, only one ship, the *Loch Broom*, was really profitable over the period, and this only to the tune of an average annual figure of £153. Her sister, the *Loch Carron*, just about broke even. The other nine vessels were loss-making, the worst performer being the *Loch Ryan* which realised an annual average loss of £1,270, registering a loss in excess of £1,000 on each of her last four voyages.

Voyage results by vessel, 1904-1911 (losses in brackets – excludes one voyage by *Loch Vennachar*)

Ship	Voyages	Total earnings (£)	Average earnings (£)
Loch Broom	8	1,223	153
Loch Carron	7	29	4 .
Loch Katrine	5	(1,304)	(261)
Loch Tay	5	(1,361)	(272)
Loch Rannoch	4	(1,262)	(316)
Loch Garry	5	(1,723)	(345)
Loch Ness	3	(1,514)	(505)
Loch Torridon	8	(4,145)	(518)
Loch Etive	7	(4,618)	(660)
Loch Ryan	4	(5,081)	(1,270)

Voyage results by year, 1904-1911 (losses in brackets – includes 1905 voyage of *Loch Vennachar*)

Year	Voyages	Total earnings (£)	Average earnings (£)
1904	7	(6,322)	(903)
1905	10	(801)	(80)
1906	10	(4,883)	(488)
1907	11	(763)	(69)
1908	9	(3,421)	(380)
1909	6	(2,185)	(364)
1910	4	(2,258)	(565)
1911	3	(821)	(274)

The worst year was 1904, when total voyage losses exceeded £6,000, and the *Loch Torridon* completed the worst single voyage of the entire period which alone contributed over £2,800 to the deficit. 1906 was only slightly better, with total losses just short of £5,000, and only one of ten completed voyages registering any profit at all (and that a miserable £148). The losses were generally registered on the line's traditional business, carrying general cargo out to Australia and wool or grain home from there. When Aitken and Lilburn sent their ships elsewhere in search of more profitable cargoes, the Loch liners actually seemed to do even worse. Apart from the loss of the *Loch Long* on its ill-fated venture into the New Caledonia nickel ore trade, the huge loss registered by the *Loch Torridon* in 1904 was partially the result of her being sent from Australia to San Francisco, where she was forced to wait almost five months for a homewards cargo, while the worst voyage of the *Loch Ryan* included an unprofitable round trip from Melbourne to East London between the normal outward and homeward legs.

Financial performance

The wealth of detail in the surviving voyage accounts allows an interesting analysis of this sorry financial record. One of the first things it shows is that the financial performance of individual vessels had little to do with their sailing performance. The traditional histories of the sailing ship tend to focus on speed and voyage times almost to the exclusion of all else. These were certainly important in the golden age of the clipper in the 1860s, and were certainly still a factor in the 1870s and early 1880s when most of the Loch fleet was built. By the turn of the century, speed no longer meant premium rates or improved attention from shippers. The *Loch Broom* and the *Loch Carron* were marginally the best performers in the fleet in terms of overall voyage times, but their status as the only two vessels to register marginally positive voyage results was due more to their greater cargo carrying capacity. The two fastest ships in the fleet, the *Loch Garry* and the *Loch Torridon*, each registered bigger average losses than the *Loch Tay*, which was one of the slowest.

One thing that was clearly a problem for the fleet as a whole was the relatively large amount of time it spent unprofitably in port. Taking the four years 1904-7 together, the Loch Line ships spent only 51% of their time at sea. Thus for almost six months of each year they were in port, either loading or actually laid up awaiting seasonal cargo. As the ships actually only earned profits by carrying cargo, these extended port times could only reduce profitability, even if costs were reduced by discharging crew or laying up away from the berth. Extended port times were a general problem for early twentieth century sailing ships, but the Loch problem was undoubtedly made worse by the trades it persisted in following. Scraping together an outward general cargo at Glasgow was often a prolonged process, while the seasonal nature of the staple homeward cargoes could mean equally long waits at Melbourne.

Carrying capacity was another problem. The three 1880s-built four-masters could lift a deadweight of 3,000 tons each, but the rest of the fleet could only manage 1,650-1,750. This was significantly less than the last generation of sailing ships built in the late 1880s and early 1890s, whose fuller hull forms produced significantly greater carrying capacity. While the Loch liners were capable of faster passages, even when reduced to barque-rig as most of them were by the time, this speed earned them little more than a few days off the provision bill, scarce compensation for reduced freight revenues.

The biggest problem for the Loch Line was simply that freight revenues had fallen in the face of increased competition and changing trade patterns. A comparison of freight revenues and operating expenses over time brings the key variables here into focus. For the purposes of this exercise, average revenues on outward and homeward voyages and average voyage costs, broken down under major expenditure headings, have been compared for two consecutive years in the early 1890s (1890-91) when the fleet was still profit-making and two consecutive years in the final loss-

making era (1906-07). No voyage records survive for the period 1897-1902, but the two years chosen before that time were the last pair in which average voyage profits were above £1,000. The two years chosen from the post 1903 period are fairly typical, including one of the worst (1906) and the best (1907) years of that miserable time. These figures make it clear that the collapse in profitability was entirely due to falling revenues. Costs were almost the same on a per voyage basis in the early 1890s and the mid-1900s, with only port charges showing a notable increase (largely balanced by slightly lower wage, food and repair bills). Revenues were steeply down, accounting entirely for the £1,500-2,000 negative swing in average voyage earnings. Homeward revenues shrunk by about 15% on average, but the real damage was done on the outward leg of each voyage, where the average fall was some 40%. Although competition had stiffened and freights rates weakened, the Loch liners were still a viable proposition carrying wool or grain back to the

Average voyage revenues and expenses, 1890-91 vs 1906-7

	1890	1891	1906	1907
Outward revenues	3,798	3,258	2,128	2,308
Homeward revenues	3,678	3,756	3,121	3,199
Average revenues	**7,474**	**7,014**	**5,248**	**5,513**
Port charges	664	625	761	752
Loading	1,149	1,060	1,241	1,079
Wages	1,220	1,251	1,186	1,181
Repairs	720	707	608	638
Food	566	485	475	424
Insurance	443	404	414	526
Claims	407	27	9	14
Advertisements	122	115	87	93
Concessions	360	383	485	339
Brokerage	604	534	470	527
Average costs	**5,871**	**5,590**	**5,737**	**5,583**
Average earnings	**1,603**	**1,424**	**(488)**	**(69)**
Operating margin	**21.4%**	**20.3%**	**-9.3%**	**-1.3%**

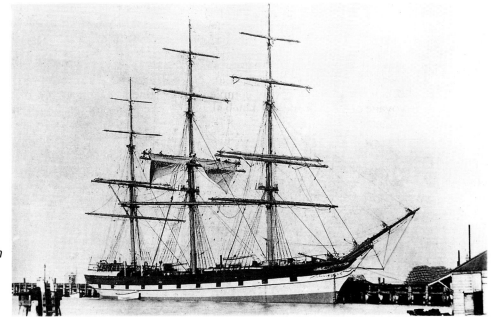

The best and worst vessels in the Loch Line fleet in terms of profitability were, respectively, the iron four-masted barque *Loch Broom* of 1885 (top) and the iron ship *Loch Ryan* of 1877 (right). *[Both: John Naylon collection]*

The iron *Loch Rannoch* dating from 1869, and barque-rigged when photographed. Unusually, she is coming to anchor under staysails and headsails only, with all square sails neatly furled. The oldest ship in the fleet, *Loch Rannoch* was the first to go when the Loch Line began to dispose of its fleet in 1907. *[John Naylon collection]*

LOCH RANNOCH

UK from Australia. This was not the case outward bound, where neither the general cargo trade nor the passenger business really justified the maintenance of a regular sailing vessel service.

The literature of the last days of commercial sail is heavily tinted with stories of cost-cutting, undertaken to maintain profits in the face of falling freights. The figures above suggest that Aitken and Lilburn did not particularly follow this path. To a certain degree the figures might be misleading. Many of the full-rigged ships in the fleet were reduced to barque rig around the turn of the century and surviving crew lists suggest that some reduction in crewing (both in terms of crew size and crew quality) was achieved. Gains here, however, were cancelled out by price pressures elsewhere. The photographic evidence is enough to suggest that considerable expense was incurred right through to the end to maintain vessels to the higher standards expected of a liner service. If this was indeed the case then the arithmetic of profit and loss reinforces the view that the Loch Line was being run on a business model that no longer made economic sense.

Last of the *Lochs*

The managers seem finally to have begun to realise that their fleet was never likely to return to profits in 1907. That year saw the first sale of what was eventually to be a complete fleet disposal. The vessel to go, the *Loch Rannoch*, was actually the oldest in the fleet although not the longest serving as she had joined in 1875, after six and a half years as Kidston's *Clanranald*. Sold to Norwegian owners, she lasted only another two years before going to German breakers. By the time she made her last trip, four other vessels had also been sold. Three of the four survivors of the initial 1869-70 building programme were disposed of in 1908-09. The *Loch Tay* and *Loch Ness* were both sold for use as coal hulks in Australian harbours, while the *Loch Lomond* was sold to the Union Shipping Company of New Zealand for possible use as a sail training ship. The three ships between them had only

registered two profitable voyages in the previous four years. The fourth disposal was the wretched *Loch Ryan*, the least profitable vessel in the fleet, which had registered aggregate losses in excess of £5,000 between 1903 and 1907. She too was destined for use as a training ship in Antipodean waters. The *Loch Lomond* lasted only a short time after her sale, disappearing with all hands on the last leg of her voyage out to New Zealand. The other three were still afloat at the outbreak of the Great War, although only the *Loch Ryan* in her new guise as the Government of Victoria training ship *John Murray* was in anything approaching seagoing condition.

The last three three-masters completed their company service in 1910-11. Of these the *Loch Katrine* was the first to go, sold after losing her fore and main masts off the South Australia coast to join her two sisters as a coal hulk. The *Loch Etive* and the *Loch Garry* both followed in 1911, each being sold straight to Italian shipbreakers. The three four-masters soldiered on alone for a while, but each was sold for further trading in 1912. The two sisters *Loch Broom* and *Loch Carron* both joined the fleet of the same Norwegian owner, while the *Loch Torridon* went to a Finnish owner under the Russian flag. All three of these ships were lost during the war, although two succumbed to marine hazard rather than the enemy. They shared this fate with the *John Murray* (ex-*Loch Ryan*), which was put back into commercial service in 1917 but wrecked on a Pacific Island in mid-1918. Thus it was actually three of the original fleet, the *Loch Katrine*, *Loch Ness* and *Loch Tay*, each of which had made its maiden voyage in 1869, which were still afloat, albeit only as coal hulks, in 1919. The *Loch Ness* was sunk as a target by the Australian Navy in 1926. The *Loch Tay* was not broken up until 1958. By this time, the *Loch Katrine* had long-since been sunk as a breakwater at Rabaul, but part of her hull was reported still to be visible and recognizable in the 1990s, a century and a quarter after her sturdy iron hull first went down the ways at Lawrie's Whiteinch shipyard.

Left: The iron ship *Loch Lomond* of 1870 at Melbourne. Note the main sky sail yard. *[John Naylon collection]*

Bottom: The steel barque *Loch Nevis* under sail. She was the last ship built for Aitken and Milburn in 1894 but was sold in 1900. *[John Naylon collection]*

Low profitability

In retrospect, it seems surprising that Aitken, Lilburn and Co. persevered as long as they did with what was obviously a failing business. Some partial explanations do suggest themselves. By the turn of the century most of the original Loch Line investors and managers were dead. The survivors or their heirs either had insufficient capital to make the leap to steam or had significant other interests attracting their attention and their money. Aitken, Lilburn and Co. operated a profitable broking business, loading cargoes for Australia on chartered tonnage and handling the Glasgow to Australia sailings of the Blue Funnel Line. With the exception of the short-lived *Loch Nevis*, investment in the sailing

fleet had ceased after 1885 and, fifteen years later, the surviving vessels might simply have been seen as a sunk cost, the operation of which did at least make a contribution to the managing business's brokerage fees. Against this background, it might simply have been a matter of carrying on until accumulated losses were too big to carry.

This said, there is evidence that the profitability of fast sailing vessels on the Australian route had reached unacceptably low levels long before the business actually sank into loss. Even the vessels added to the fleet in the late 1870s and early 1880s seem never really to have paid for themselves. Voyage accounts survive for the period from the mid-1870s to the mid 1890s, and then for the period from 1903 until 1911. Using these as a basis for estimating the profitability of individual vessels provides some interesting, if rather depressing results. Two examples are covered here.

The *Loch Etive* entered service in early 1878. Details of her contract price have not been traced, but prices being quoted by other Clyde shipbuilders at the time for similar vessels were generally just above £15 per gross ton, which would suggest that she cost about £20,000. Results survive for voyages 1-18 and 25-31 of her 31-voyage career. If we assume that the voyage results for the missing voyages 19-24 were the same as the average result for all the other voyages, then the *Loch Etive* only earned a total of £10,293 during her 32-year career. Given that the missing voyage results fall in the generally less profitable second half of this career, the figure seems unlikely to be an overestimate. There is no charge for depreciation in the voyage accounts, so it would appear that the *Loch Etive* only returned about half of her original purchase cost to her shareholders, with the £1,350 realised on her sale for scrap making little material difference to the equation.

The picture does not look any better for the newer and larger *Loch Broom*, which entered service in 1885 at a cost likely to have been in the vicinity of £30,000. In her case results survive for voyages 1-10 and 17-24. The impact of the process of estimation for

the missing results might be more of a distortion than was the case for the *Loch Etive* as the missing voyages make up a larger proportion of the whole and occurred roughly at the mid-point of her career, but the results are once again so poor as to make it seem highly unlikely that the *Loch Broom* ever came close to covering the cost of her original investment. Estimated total voyage results for her 24-year career come only to £12,313, and adding the £3-4,000 for which she is likely to have been sold is only sufficient to move the total return up to just over half of her likely purchase cost.

British sailing vessels could produce reasonable profits into the last decade of the nineteenth century. The Scottish four-masted barque *Queen Margaret*, for example, earned total voyage profits of just over £15,000 on her first seven voyages between 1893 and 1902. Indeed, had sailing ships not still been a viable proposition, it would be difficult to understand why so many large square-riggers were still being built in the early 1890s. These, however, were different vessels operated on different principles from the Loch liners. The latter, denied the added cargo capacity necessary to maximise bulk freight carriage or the flexibility to seek cargo where it was most profitable, seem to have been a wasting asset long before their owners finally accepted the fact.

Durability

However unimpressive the economic verdict on the business, it seems only fair to end by paying credit to the immense durability of the ships themselves and the men who commanded them. The four survivors of the company's 1869-70 building programme averaged 39 years in company colours. The *Loch Katrine*, the first to enter the fleet in September 1869, was only taken out of service after being dismasted off South Australia in April 1910 following 40½ years of continuous service. The last Loch vessel actually to serve under sail, the *Loch Ryan*, had been afloat for almost exactly the same amount of time when she was finally wrecked in the South Pacific in 1918. Mention has already been made of Captain Stainton Clarke's

long sojourn as master of the *Loch Carron*. Other men performed similar feats of endurance. Captain James Horne, for example, took over the *Loch Garry* in 1885 and remained in command until her final sale in 1910, when he retired from the sea at the age of 75. The Canadian historian Frederick William Wallace famously coined the phrase 'Wooden Ships and Iron Men' to describe the sailing fleets of Atlantic Canada. The masters of the Loch Line were clearly no less iron themselves for having iron hulls beneath their feet!
To be continued

Above: The iron ship *Loch Katrine* of 1869, the remains of whose hull was still visible in the 1990s. *[John Naylon collection]*

Opposite: *Loch Etive* in the Clyde. A splendid-looking ship, she could not have been a good investment for her owners. *[William Robertson, John Naylon collection]*

Below: *Loch Garry* of 1875, seen at Sydney, was another Loch Line ship with a long serving master. *[John Naylon collection]*

THE BLUE FUNNEL TRANS-PACIFIC SERVICE
Peter L. Ruddle

A personal introduction

When I started working for Alfred Holt as a junior engineer in early 1958 the first few days were a whirl of activity, finding accommodation, medical examinations, visits to the tailor to get measured for uniforms, vaccinations, registering at the pool and getting issued with an identity card and discharge book. The accommodation was at the Holt's hostel in Birkenhead Park - Odyssey House - the one and only time I stayed there. It was very formal compared to the accommodation provided by the landladies along Conway Street opposite Birkenhead Park.

On the fourth day I and another, more senior, engineer were on a train on our way to Amsterdam as reliefs for a ship arriving there as the first port of call from a deep-sea voyage. I was to join a ship as seventh engineer without ever spending any time on the famed Holt's shore gang. The ship was the *Automedon* (8,236/1949) built by Vickers-Armstrongs Ltd. in Newcastle for the Ocean Steamship Co. Ltd. and with an eight-cylinder two-stroke double-acting Burmeister & Wain-type engine. We were waiting on the dockside when she arrived. Only two of the seven engineers were relieved so there was a lot of disappointment. The *Automedon* was returning home after a lengthy round-the-world voyage that was a legacy of a once-regular service that was taken over by Blue Funnel Line with the acquisition of China Mutual and later Indra Line.

Consequently, my first trip to sea was from Amsterdam to Hamburg then to Glasgow before arriving at Gladstone Dock, Liverpool to start unloading.

Unfortunately, bad weather around the north of Scotland and the effects of my first ever smallpox vaccination helped to make a part of this trip a very unpleasant experience. The *Automedon* was subject to a complete engine overhaul after arrival in Liverpool and, following discharge of the cargo, was towed over to Birkenhead and berthed in the Vittoria Dock while work continued and then to West Float prior to return to Vittoria Dock to start loading for a voyage to the Far East. I lived on board the *Automedon* for the whole period until the deep-sea crew arrived and I was assigned to work on other vessels as part of the shore gang.

The first trans-Pacific sailings

The acquisition of the China Mutual Shippers' Steam Navigation Co. Ltd. in 1902 gave Blue Funnel a trans-Pacific service, which allowed them to open the round-the-world service to which I was introduced by *Automedon*. According to US immigration records, the first Blue Funnel ship to arrive in Puget Sound after the acquisition of China Mutual was one of the latter's former ships, the *Hyson* (6,608/1899), recorded in October 1902 and again in April 1903. *Calchas* (6,748/1899) was there in January 1904 and another ex-China

Two *Bellerophon* class ships, *Tyndareus* and *Protesilaus* at the Seattle wharf of the Dodwell Dock and Warehouse Company in the early 1930s. The *Tyndareus*, right, as one of the later members of the class, has a cross beam on the aft goalpost mast. *[Puget Sound Maritime Historical Society]*

Mutual ship, *Yang-tsze* (6,457/1899) in December 1904. After that there are visits from ships from both China Mutual and Holt's fleets, the latter including *Calchas* (6,748/1899), *Telemachus* (7,450/1902) and *Stentor* (6,773/1899). Vessels turned up at Seattle at least monthly. It is interesting to note that Glen Line's *Glenogle* (3,750/1882) visited in May 1900, August 1902, January 1903 and August 1904.

Beginning with the *Bellerophon* (8,918/1906), a class of ship was specifically designed and built for this service with goal post masts for handling the large

Above: *Tyndareus* at the Handford Street Pier grain elevator in Seattle during the 1930s.*[Puget Sound Maritime Historical Society]*

Below: *Ixion* underway in Seattle harbour in 1932. The portholes for the 'tween deck accommodation can be clearly seen. The *Ixion* and *Tyndareus* were part of the third batch of the *Bellerophon* class, and were the first with the additional tie beam on the after goal post masts.*[Puget Sound Maritime Historical Society]*

logs that were exported from the Pacific Northwest to Asia and with 'tween deck accommodation for immigrant passengers. The *Bellerophon* class were constructed in batches over a period of 18 years with each batch being larger than its predecessor. The *Bellerophon* (8,918/1906), *Cyclops* (8,998/1906) and the *Protesilaus* (9,547/1910) were 485 feet in length. The *Ixion* (10,224/1912), *Tyndareus* (11,347/1916) and the *Achilles* (1920/11,426) measured 507 feet. Nearly all of the class were twin screw with two triple-expansion engines supplied with steam at 200 psi from two coal-fired double-ended Scotch boilers. Work on the *Achilles* was suspended during the First World War, and the delay probably meant that Holts could, for the first time, specify steam turbine machinery. The later and slightly larger *Philoctetes* (11,466/1922) also had reduction-geared turbines.

During the Second World War the *Tyndareus* was used as a troopship continuing her tradition of the 'bulk' carriage of personnel. After the war she was converted for use as a pilgrim ship and continued carrying large numbers of passengers from South East Asia to Jeddah. When I last saw the *Tyndareus* in Singapore in 1960 she was still employed in this service although broken up in Hong Kong soon after when Holts acquired the *Empire Orwell* and employed her as the *Gunung Djati* in the pilgrim trade. *Achilles* was sold to the Admiralty in 1941 and employed as the destroyer depot ship HMS *Blenheim* during the Second World War. She never returned to civilian service, being broken up at Barrow-in-Furness in 1948.

Above: *Cyclops* at the Dodwell company's wharf. One of the original batch of *Bellerophons*, *Cyclops* entered service in the same year as the name ship. In this photograph she has a casing around the lower section of the funnel. The goal post masts were fitted to facilitate the carriage of logs in the transPacific trade, but here *Cyclop's* gear is handling sawn timber, whilst a tug waits to move the lumber scows.

Cyclops had two encounters with U-boats during the First World War, escaping both times, but was less fortunate during the Second World War. She was torpedoed by U 123 125 miles off the coast of New England on 11th January 1942 whilst on a voyage from Hong Kong and Auckland to the UK via Halifax. *[Puget Sound Maritime Historical Society]*

Opposite page top: Looking aft from the forecastle of *Cyclops*. This was clearly taken on a different occasion to the photograph above, as the casing has been removed from the funnel although the skirt is still in place. The ship's name can be seen, mounted above the bridge.*[Puget Sound Maritime Historical Society]*

Opposite bottom: Looking forward on the *Cyclop's* deck, from behind the rear samson post and just forward of the aft accommodation house. The cargo being loaded with the *Cyclop's* own gear appears to be steel rails, and one of the railcars can be identified as belonging to the Union Railroad of Pittsburgh, Pennsylvania. Note the hatch beams lying on the deck, and the clutter of slings and dunnage. The casing skirt round the funnel is still in place in this view. *[Puget Sound Maritime Historical Society]*

Chinese immigrants

Along with the cargoes carried in both directions across the Pacific Ocean there was, in the 19th and early 20th century, a thriving service for the carriage of Chinese migrants drawn by the prospect of gold. However, few if any struck it rich, and they mostly laboured in the mines, railroads, farms and canneries with many settling in the area around South Washington Street in Seattle. As more and more Chinese moved into the area the immigrants established their own community. One group collectively invested money to build the Kong Yick buildings that are still the core of Seattle's Chinatown district. One immigrant, 'Henry' Mar Fook Hing, had arrived in Port Townsend from Guandong in South China just after the turn of the century. He moved to Seattle in 1909 and earned money doing odd jobs around the neighbourhood. Within a few years he had saved enough to think of opening his own business and established an importing and exporting company around 1912 to cater for the needs of the Chinese residents of the area. This company, The Yick Fung Company, specialized in importing the foods and speciality goods from China that were needed by the local population and restaurants.

Many of the immigrants who had spent their lives labouring on farms and railroads wanted to return to their homeland as they grew older to see their families and to die in their ancestral homes. In 1918 a representative of the Dodwell Steamship Company asked Henry Mar if he would be the sole agent to handle this returning passenger trade. Dodwells had previously been the agents for the China Mutual trans-Pacific services and following the acquisition became the agent for Blue Funnel Line passenger and cargo services from Hong Kong to the Pacific Northwest.

In addition to acting as the agent for the steerage passenger trade, Henry Mar recognized the opportunity for other business as an extension of the passenger agent activities. The upper rooms of the Yick Fung Company store were turned into accommodation to provide lodging for 25 to 30 men who were to be some of the passengers on the next departing vessel. They were provided with two meals a day. Naturally the passengers shopped for gifts to take back to their families and supplies for the journey. For items that Henry Mar could not supply to them he started a service to take them shopping and to transport them and their baggage to and from the ship. A sideline of the transport service was a taxi service to take the 'guests' to gambling places and places of prostitution. Henry Mar was anxious that his own sons be well established in businesses of their own and eventually each of them became responsible for a part of the growing business, accommodating and feeding the passengers, transportation, gifts and supplies, hair cutting and the trading company and passenger agency. The passenger agency and trading company came to one of his sons, Jimmy Mar. Jimmy is still running the business though it is now more in the form of a museum as a part of the Chinatown International District historical museum.

Catering for the immigrants

Most of the steerage passengers were transported on the *Tyndareus* and the *Protesilaus* with Yick Fung normally having from 90 to 100 passengers ready to sail back home every month. In 1928 Jimmy, then 14 years old, and his elder brother sailed on the *Tyndareus*, being sent back to Canton to learn Chinese. They stayed there for three years and returned home to Seattle on the same vessel. Accommodation for the returning immigrants was sparse. Bunks were stacked eight to ten feet high in the 'tween decks space. Blue Funnel provided basic mattresses with each bunk but the passengers were required to provide their own sheets, blankets and pillows. The kitchen crew consisted of two cooks and two helpers and the steerage passengers were fed three meals a day at 8:00 am, noon and a dinner at 6:00 am. Each of the ships had its own commissary with live chickens and pigs kept on deck and fresh fruits and vegetables, beef and other fresh meats were stored in the ship's lockers and these supplies were replenished at each port of call on the way to Hong Kong. After departing from Seattle the ship would call at Victoria and Vancouver prior to crossing the Pacific and then call at four or five ports around the coast of Japan for unloading and loading cargo prior to arrival in Hong Kong. The ship's passenger accommodation was reserved for Caucasians but Jimmy Mar and his brother, being company agents, were accommodated in the purser's cabin and were allowed to eat in the ship's dining room.

The trans-Pacific service was suspended at the start of the Second World War and the last ship to depart from Seattle for Asia was the *Tyndareus*. Jimmy Mar was drafted into the US army and went away to war. Civil war in China and the communist takeover of the mainland eliminated the possibility of Chinese nationals returning to their homeland in large numbers and the immigrant service was no longer required.

Opposite: Ash is piled on deck awaiting disposal once *Cyclops* puts to sea. Note also the bellows-operated forge for metalworking.

Below: The boiler room showing the stoker's workplace. Firebricks are stacked to one side, and there is much slag and ash on the deck, plus an upturned wheelbarrow. The fittings to the left appear to be be part of the drafting arrangements: 'Open' and 'Shut' are embossed on the diagonal pipework. *[Both: Puget Sound Maritime Historical Society]*

The photographs

The on board photographs were taken whilst the *Cyclops* was loading cargo at the wharf of the Dodwell Dock and Warehouse Company in Seattle. They show the deck area while cargo is being worked, the engine room and the Chinese engine room hands' accommodation. For someone like myself who sailed on modern Blue Funnel ships it is difficult to appreciate the poor conditions and hardship for those that worked in the boiler room.

Opposite top: A view across the front of the main engines showing the valve gear eccentric shafts, auxiliary pumps and the condenser.

Opposite bottom: one of the tail shaft tunnels.

This page, top: The Chinese crew's quarters down aft.

Middle: Another view of the crew's quarters.

Bottom right: Chinese cooks looking out of the galley door,

Bottom left: Food storage area for the Chinese crew.

All: *Puget Sound Maritime Historical Society.*

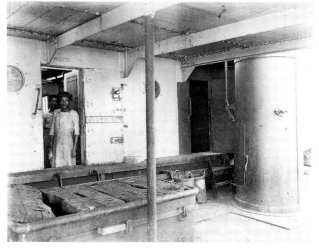

Top: *Edenor* shortly after her launch. [G.R.Scott collection]
Middle: Some of the crew and perhaps some shipyard workers pose for a photograph. [G.R.Scott collection]
Right: The first arch deck vessel, *Edenor* later became familiar on the UK east coast as Charrington's *Camden*. This view emphasizes her negative sheer. [Ships in Focus]
Opposite page top: *Edenor* appears to have been photographed many times, especially in her later life as *Arkadia*. [Stig Lothner, Helsinki]
Lower: *Sheaf Arrow* - the attachment on the bow dates the photograph to the First World War period. [Ivor Rooke collection]

THE ARCH DECK STEAMERS Part 2

The Archers*

*'The Archers' include David Burrell who began the project, Harold Appleyard, Malcolm Cooper, Roy Fenton, Stig Lothner, Kevin O'Donoghue, Bill Schell and George Scott.

Arch deck vessels in chronological order of launch

1. EDENOR/CAMDEN/JULIETTE/ MARJA-LIISA NURMINEN/ ARKADIA

O.N. 136736 1,425g 863n 240.2 x 34.2 x 20.1 feet
T. 3-cyl. by MacColl and Pollock Ltd., Sunderland; 148 NHP, 740 IHP, 9.5 knots.
2.3.1911: Launched by Osbourne, Graham and Co., Sunderland (Yard No.156).
4.1911: Completed for Gronquist, Bryan and Co., Newcastle-upon-Tyne who placed the ship under the Swedish flag under the ownership of Rederiaktiebolaget Edenor (Tuve Persson, manager) Helsingborg, Sweden as EDENOR.
4.1.1915: Registered in the ownership of Gardner, Locket and Hinton Ltd., London as CAMDEN.
21.10.1922: Owners became Charrington, Gardner, Lockett and Co. Ltd., London.
22.12.1930: Owners became the Charrington Steamship Co. Ltd. (Charrington, Gardner, Lockett and Co. Ltd., managers), London.
21.11.1938: Sold to Angel, Son and Co. Ltd., Cardiff.

13.4.1939: Sold to Laiva O/Y Fennia Steamship Co. Ltd. (John Nurminen O/Y, managers), Helsinki, Finland and renamed JULIETTE. Chartered to F.W. Moorsom and Co. Ltd., Cardiff, who were the main shareholders in the owning company.
3.9.1940: Renamed LIISA after completion of charter.
21.10.1947: Renamed MARJA-LIISA NURMINEN.
4.3.1948: Owners became John Nurminen O/Y.
28.6.1949: Sold to Laivaisännistöyhtiö Arkadia (Polttoaine Osuuskunta, manager), Helsinki and renamed ARKADIA.
1951: Trransferred to Etela-Suomen Laiva O/Y (Polttoaine Osuuskunta, manager), Helsinki.
26.8.1959: Sold to Sorema S.p.r.l. for demolition.
8.10.1959: Arrived at Hemixem, Belgium in tow of the Polish salvage tug KORAL (1,225/1959) for breaking.

2. SHEAF ARROW

O.N. 133510 2,094g 1,175n 278.9 x 40.3 x 22.6 feet
T. 3-cyl. by MacColl and Pollock Ltd., Sunderland; 330 NHP, 1,700 IHP, 10 knots.
18.6.1912: Launched by the Blyth Shipbuilding and Dry Dock Co. Ltd., Blyth (Yard No. 166).
8.1912: Completed
1.8.1912: Registered in the ownership of the Sheaf Arrow Steam Shipping Co. Ltd. (W.A. Souter and Co., managers), Newcastle-upon-Tyne as SHEAF ARROW.
4.1.1915: Owners became the Sheaf Steam Shipping Co. Ltd. (W.A. Souter and Co., managers), Newcastle-upon-Tyne.
6.9.1933: Sold to Thomas W. Ward Ltd., Sheffield and broken up at Inverkeithing.

Left: *Luis Pidal*, built as *Thyra Menier* approaching Bristol. *[J.& M.Clarkson collection]*

Middle: Now named *Empire Conderton* loading in South Wales circa 1947. *[Hansen 994/1096 , National Museums and Galleries of Wales]*

Bottom: Under the drops for another fuel cargo - now as *Marchmont* in 1948. *[Hansen 2381/2432, National Museums and Galleries of Wales]*

Opposite top: Still as the *Marchmont* but now sporting some white paint. *[G.R.Scott collection]*

**3. THYRA MENIER/LUIS PIDAL/
BELLINI/BOLLAN/LINA FISSER/
EMPIRE CONDERTON/
MARCHMONT/IRENE M**
O.N. 127100 1,457g 794n 240.0 x 36.1 x
20.1 feet
T. 3-cyl. by G.T. Grey, South Shields;
146 NHP.
13.8.1912: Launched by the Blyth
Shipbuilding Co. Ltd., Blyth (Yard No.
168).
9.1912: Completed for the Donald
Steamship Co. Ltd. (Thomas L. Evans,
manager), Bristol as THYRA MENIER.
1917: Sold to F. Lecoeuvre
(Compagnie Royale Asturienne des
Mines), Tonnay Charente, France and
renamed LUIS PIDAL.
1919: Transferred to Compagnie
Royale Asturienne des Mines, Ant-
werp, Belgium.
1925: Sold to Puglisi e Tomasini,
Catania, Italy and renamed BELLINI.
12.11.1928: Sold to Aug. Bolten, Wm.
Miller's Nachfolger, Hamburg, Germany and renamed BOLLAN.
28.12.1935: Transferred to China
Rhederei A.G., Hamburg.
13.1.1936: Sold to Reunert & Co.,
G.m.b.H. (Fisser & v. Doornum),
Hamburg.
16.1.1936: Renamed LINA FISSER.
4.1.1939: Transferred to Fisser & van
Doornum Reederei G.m.b.H., Hamburg.
29.7.1945: Arrived Methil having
been taken over by the Allies.
1945: Transferred to Ministry of
Transport (Alliance Maritime Transport Co., Ltd., mgrs.), London and
renamed EMPIRE CONDERTON.
1946: Transferred to the Ministry of
Transport, London.

1947: Sold to Marchmont Steamship
Co. Ltd. (J.P. Hadoulis, manager),
London and renamed MARCHMONT.
1952: Sold to Mina Shipping Co. Ltd.
(A. Moschakis, Ltd.), London and
renamed IRENE M.
1955: Sold to Tampa Shipping, Ltd.,
Halifax, Nova Scotia (Frierson,
Robinson Steamship Co., Tampa,
Florida, USA, managers).
15.7.1957: Arrived at Sorel, P.Q. to be
broken up by Marine Industries, Ltd.

**4. PENNYBURN/GLENMAVIS/
ACADIAN**
O.N. 133533 1,686g 1,055n 250.0 x
42.5 x 17.4 feet
T. 3-cyl. by Richardsons, Westgarth
and Co. Ltd., Middlesbrough; 96 NHP,
750 IHP, 8½ knots.

19.4.1913: Launched by the North of
Ireland Shipbuilding Co. Ltd., London-
derry (Yard No. 55) as PENNYBURN,
probably for their own account.
6.1913: Completed for James Playfair
and H. W. Richardson, Midland,
Ontario, Canada as GLENMAVIS.
1916: Transferred to Great Lakes
Transportation Co. Ltd. (James
Playfair, manager), Midland, Ontario.
1926: Sold to the George Hall Coal and
Shipping Corporation, Montreal,
Canada.
1926: Transferred to Steamships, Ltd.
(Canada Steamship Lines Ltd.),
Montreal.
1927: Transferred to Canada Steamship Lines Ltd., Montreal and renamed
ACADIAN.
10.1959: Broken up in Kingston
Drydock, Kingston, Ontario.

Glenmavis, on her first voyage. *[G.R.Scott collection]*

Honoreva, a trial's view which shows off the arch deck. Note the maple leaf on the funnel. *[G.R.Scott collection]*

5. GLENFOYLE
O.N. 135641 1,680g 1,051n 250.0 x
42.5 x 17.4 feet
T. 3-cyl. by MacColl and Pollock,
Sunderland; 97 NHP, 750 IHP, 8½ knots.
19.4.1913: Launched by the North of
Ireland Shipbuilding Co. Ltd., London-
derry (Yard No. 56).
26.8.1913: Registered in the owner-
ship of Trevisa Clark, Liverpool as
GLENFOYLE.
5.1.1914: Sold to James Playfair,
Midland, Ontario and Harry W.
Richardson, Kingston, Ontario,
Canada (Swan, Hunter and Wigham
Richardson, Wallsend-on-Tyne,
managers).
22.3.1916: Transferred to the Great
Lakes Transportation Co. Ltd. (James
Playfair, manager), Midland, Ontario.
4.1917: Requisitioned by the Royal
Navy as a Q-ship, pennant number
Y3.1235, operating under the names
DONLEVON and STONECROP.
18.9.1917: Torpedoed and sunk by
the German submarine U 43 about 65
miles south west of Mizen Head,
Ireland whilst on service as a Q-ship.
The commander of the Q-ship believed
he had sunk the submarine, wrongly
identified as U 88, but it escaped.
18.2.1920: Register closed.

6. HONOREVA/ASTURIENNE
O.N. 134700 1,452g 867n 240.5 x 36.2
x 20.0 feet
T. 3-cyl. by George T. Grey, South
Shields; 111 NHP, 675 IHP, 9¼ knots.
1.8.1913: Launched by Osbourne,
Graham and Co., Sunderland (Yard No.
173).
8.9.1913: Registered in the ownership
of the Donald Steamship Co. Ltd.
(Thomas L. Evans, manager), Bristol as
HONOREVA.
8.1.1916: Owners became the Donald
Steamship Co. Ltd. (Thomas L. Evans,

manager), Montreal, Canada on the
winding-up of the original owning
company.
17.8.1916: Sold to the Ontario Transportation and Pulp Co. Ltd., Thorold,
Ontario, Canada.
24.8.1916: Sold to the Great Lakes
Transportation Co. Ltd. (James
Playfair, manager), Midland, Ontario.
3.1917: Sold to Compagnie Royale
Asturienne des Mines, Paris, France
and renamed ASTURIENNE.
24.7.1917: Wrecked on underwater
obstruction south east of Cape
Finisterre whilst on a voyage from
Aviles to Lisbon with a cargo of bar
iron. This was regarded as a partial
war loss, as a the captain was avoiding
a German submarine.

**7. PENSACOLA/CLAPTON/SAIMA/
DANAPRIS**
O.N. 135906 2,092g 1,268n 279.3 x
40.3 x 22.6 feet
T. 3-cyl. by Richardsons, Westgarth and
Co. Ltd., Sunderland; 206 NHP, 950
IHP, 9¼ knots.
27.5.1914: Launched by Osbourne,
Graham and Co., Sunderland (Yard No. 182).
15.7.1914: Registered in the owner-
ship of Furness, Withy and Co. Ltd.,
West Hartlepool as PENSACOLA.
11.10.1921: Sold to Arthur Capel and
Co. Ltd., Newcastle-upon-Tyne.
14.8.1923: Sold to H. Harrison (Ship-
ping) Ltd. (Harold Harrison, manager),
London.
21.9.1923: Renamed CLAPTON.
1924: Sold to D/S A/S Saima
(Bregmann & Hammer A/S, managers),
Bergen, Norway and renamed SAIMA.
1927: Manager becomes Erling
Hammer.
1929: Manager becomes D. Martens
Nielsen.
1936: Sold to S. Synodinos

(Synodinos Brothers, managers),
Piraeus, Greece and renamed
DANAPRIS.
27.4.1941: Bombed and sunk at
Piraeus.
Refloated but subsequently wrecked at
Chalkis.

8. DUCKBRIDGE
O.N. 133561 1,491g 897n 240.0 x 36.2
x 20.1 feet
T. 3-cyl. built in 1905 by Schomer &
Jensen, Tonsberg, Denmark; 110 NHP,
700 IHP, 9 knots.
25.6.1914: Launched by Craig, Taylor
and Co. Ltd., Stockton-on-Tees (Yard
No. 163).
8.1914: Completed.
12.8.1914: Registered in the ownership of the Duckbridge Steam Shipping
Co. Ltd. (Thomas L. Weiss, manager),
Newcastle-upon-Tyne as
DUCKBRIDGE.
22.2.1916: Mined and sunk six miles
north of Straithie Point whilst on a
voyage from Cardiff with a cargo of coal.
4.4.1916: Register closed.

9. BEDALE
O.N. 135910 2,107g 1,269n 279.0 x
40.3 x 22.6 feet
T. 3-cyl. by Richardsons, Westgarth
and Co. Ltd., Sunderland; 205 NHP, 900
IHP, 9 knots.
10.7.1914: Launched by the North of
Ireland Shipbuilding Co. Ltd., London-
derry (Yard No. 59)
12.8.1914: Registered in the ownership of Furness, Withy and Co. Ltd.,
West Hartlepool as BEDALE.
6.10.1917: Torpedoed and sunk by
the German submarine U 96, 25 miles
south east by south of Mine Head
whilst on a voyage from Cardiff to
Berehaven with a cargo of coal.
19.10.1917: Register closed.

Top: *Pensacola*, probably when new. *[G.R.Scott collection]*
Bottom: *Pensacola* as *Saima*, arriving Preston. *[J.& M.Clarkson, G.R.Scott collection]*

10. ALTO
O.N. 133581 2,266g 1,303n 287.0 x
40.6 x 22.8 feet
T. 3-cyl. by Richardsons, Westgarth
and Co. Ltd.,Sunderland; 158 NHP,
1,200 IHP, 10 knots.
30.11.1915: Launched by the North of
Ireland Shipbuilding Co. Ltd., Londonderry (Yard No. 64).
8.2.1916: Registered in the ownership
of the Pelton Steamship Co. Ltd.
(Robert S. Gardiner, manager),
Newcastle-upon-Tyne as ALTO.
10.2.1916: Completed.

16.7.1916: Mined and sunk in the
North Sea about four miles off
Kessingland, Suffolk whilst on a
voyage from Rouen to the Tyne in
ballast. The mine had been laid earlier
that day by the German submarine
UC 1.
2.8.1916: Register closed.

11. THIRLMERE/ESKMERE

O.N. 137514 2,293g 1,216n 287.2 x 40.1 x 22.8 feet
T. 3-cyl. by MacColl and Pollock, Sunderland; 1,250 IHP, 10 knots.
10.4.1916: Launched by the North of Ireland Shipbuilding Co. Ltd., London-derry (Yard No. 66) as THIRLMERE.
7.1916: Completed.
7.7.1916: Registered in the ownership of the Bromport Steamship Co. Ltd. (Harold R. Greenhalgh, manager), Liverpool as ESKMERE.
13.10.1917: Torpedoed and sunk by the German submarine UC 75, 15 miles west north west of South Stack, Anglesey whilst on a voyage from Belfast to Barry in ballast.
3.10.1917: Register closed.

12. ARNEWOOD

O.N. 139160 2,259g 1,295n 287.2 x 40.6 x 22.8 feet
T. 3-cyl. by MacColl and Pollock Ltd., Sunderland; 158 NHP, 1,250 IHP, 10 knots.
16.8.1916: Launched by the North of Ireland Shipbuilding Co. Ltd., London-derry (Yard No. 65).
10.1916: Completed.
16.10.1916: Registered in the owner-ship of William France, Fenwick and Co. Ltd., London as ARNEWOOD.
13.12.1917: Mined and sunk four miles east south east of Sleat Point, Skye whilst on a voyage from Barry with a cargo of coal. The mine had been laid by the German submarine U 78.
15.2.1918: Register closed.

13. SHEAF DON

O.N. 133593 2,172g 1,226n 279.0 x 40.3 x 22.9 feet
T. 3-cyl. by MacColl and Pollock Ltd., Sunderland; 330 NHP, 1,700 IHP, 11 knots.
26.10.1916: Launched by the Blyth Shipbuilding Co. Ltd., Blyth (Yard No. 179).

Launched as *Thirlmere* this ship actually went to sea as *Eskmere*. *[Nigel Farrell collection]*

2.3.1917: Registered in the ownership of the Sheaf Steam Shipping Co. Ltd. (William A. Souter and Co., managers), Newcastle-upon-Tyne as SHEAF DON.
23.2.1926: Wrecked on Finsboerne Rock, Langesund whilst on a voyage from the Tyne to Skien with a cargo of coal.
27.3.1926: Register closed.

14. SAINT PAUL/LEOPOLD D'OR

2,300g 1,219n 287.2 x 40.6 x 22.8 feet
T. 3-cyl. by the Clyde Shipbuilding and Engineering Co. Ltd., Port Glas-gow; 229 NHP.
27.10.1916: Launched by the North of Ireland Shipbuilding Co. Ltd., Londonderry (Yard No. 67).
2.1917: Completed for L. Ballande fils ainé, Bordeaux, France as SAINT PAUL.
1918: Renamed LEOPOLD D'OR.
26.4.1918: Torpedoed and sunk by the German submarine UB48, 57 miles north west of San Pietro, Tyrrhenian Sea.

15. SHEAF GARTH/BRAMWELL/GLENDINNING

O.N. 145456 1,927g 1,077n 260.5 x 38.7 x 22.3 feet
T. 3-cyl. by MacColl and Pollock Ltd., Sunderland; 245 NHP, 1,550 IHP, 11 knots.
10.3.1921: Launched by the Blyth Shipbuilding Co. Ltd., Blyth (Yard No. 222).
9.1921: Completed.
7.10.1921: Registered in the owner-ship of the Sheaf Steam Shipping Co. Ltd. (William A. Souter and Co., managers), Newcastle-upon-Tyne as SHEAF GARTH.
22.10.1937: Sold to Angel, Son and Co. Ltd. (Claude Angel, manager), Cardiff.
22.10.1937: Renamed BRAMWELL.
22.4.1940: Sold to George Gibson and Co. Ltd., Leith.
27.5.1940: Renamed GLENDINNING.
5.7.1944: Torpedoed and sunk by the German submarine *U 953* in position 50.32 north by 00.22 west whilst on a voyage from the Normandy beachhead to London in ballast
21.11.1944: Register closed.

Bramwell, completed by the Blyth Shipbuilding Co.Ltd. at Blyth in 1921 as *Sheaf Garth*. *[Roy Fenton collection]*

16. ELEVEEN/GORDONIA/ BELLWYN/ASTROLOGER
O.N. 145498 1,687g 969n 245.3 x 37.3 x 22.3 feet
T. 3-cyl. by Cooper and Greig Ltd., Dundee; 141 NHP, 1,050 IHP, 10¼ knots.
9.9.1922: Launched by the Burntisland Shipbuilding Co. Ltd., Burntisland (Yard No. 118).
28.9.1922: Registered in the ownership of the Monkseaton Steamship Co. Ltd. (Edward L. Andersen, manager), Newcastle-upon-Tyne as ELEVEEN.
5.10.1922: Completed.
4.4.1927: Sold to the Swanston Steamship Co. Ltd. (William S. Swanston, trading as W. Swanston and Sons, managers), Newcastle-upon-Tyne.
11.11.1935: Manager became William G. Gordon, Newcastle-upon-Tyne.
16.12.1935: Sold to the Gordonia Steamship Co. Ltd. (William G. Gordon, trading as J.S. Gordon and Co., managers), Newcastle-upon-Tyne.
26.11.1935: Renamed GORDONIA.

25.10.1937: Sold to the Dillwyn Steamship Co. Ltd. (Claude Angel, trading as Angel, Son and Co. Ltd., managers), Cardiff.
27.10.1937: Renamed BELLWYN.
7.9.1938: Manager became Frederick A. Rees, trading as Stockwood, Rees and Co. Ltd., Swansea.
2.5.1940: Sold to George Gibson and Co. Ltd., Leith.
11.6.1940: Renamed ASTROLOGER.
7.11.1940: Beached near Barrow Beacon, Thames Estuary after being attacked by German aircraft in Barrow Deep, in position 51.32 north by 01.06 east whilst on a voyage from Leith to London with a cargo of wheat.
15.11.1940: Wreck damaged during a gale and abandoned.
26.2.1941: Register closed.

17. MARJORIE S./COURCELLES/ RUCKINGE/MORTLAKE/ STANLAKE
O.N. 145510 1,742g 981n 253.0 x 37.2 x 22.0 feet

T. 3-cyl. by Swan, Hunter and Wigham Richardson Ltd., Newcastle-upon-Tyne; 215 NHP, 1,200 IHP, 10½ knots.
1923: Launched by Swan, Hunter and Wigham Richardson Ltd., Newcastle-upon-Tyne (Yard No 1193).
9.3.1923: Registered in the ownership of Swan, Hunter and Wigham Richardson Ltd. (Monkseaton Steamship Co. Ltd., manager), Newcastle-upon-Tyne as MARJORIE S.
13.9.1923: Sold to the Monkseaton Steamship Co. Ltd., Newcastle-upon-Tyne.
12.11.1923: Manager became Edward L. Anderson.
28.11.1925: Manager became Francis J. Culley, Wallsend-on-Tyne.
1.1928: Sold to Compagnie des Affreteurs Francais, Rouen, France and renamed COURCELLES.
14.11.1929: Registered in the ownership of Constants (South Wales) Ltd. (Martin Constant, manager), London as RUCKINGE.

Top: *Eleveen. [G.R.Scott collection]*
Above: *Marjorie S of 1922. [G.R.Scott collection]*

10.12.1936: Sold to Watts, Watts and Co. Ltd., London.
14.12.1936: Renamed MORTLAKE.
28.12.1936: Owners became the Watts Shipping Co. Ltd., London.
27.6.1938: Sold to the Stanhope Steamship Co. Ltd. (Jack A. Billmeir, manager), London.
21.7.1938: Renamed STANLAKE.
14.4.1943: Torpedoed and sunk by the German E-boats S121, S82 and S90 12 miles from the Lizard Head whilst on a voyage from Portland to Barry in ballast.
28.5.1943: Register closed.

18. MURIE S/LOLITA/LOLITA A
O.N. 145513 1,701g 981n 245.6 x 37.2 x 22.3 feet
T. 3-cyl. by Swan, Hunter and Wigham Richardson Ltd., Newcastle-upon-Tyne; 215 NHP, 1,200 IHP, 10½ knots.
16.2.1923: Launched by Swan, Hunter and Wigham Richardson Ltd., Newcastle-upon-Tyne (Yard No 1201).
14.4.1923: Registered in the ownership of the Monkseaton Steamship Co. Ltd. (Edward L. Anderson, manager), Newcastle-upon-Tyne as MURIE S.
28.11.1925: Manager became Francis J. Culley, Wallsend-on-Tyne.
2.1.1929: Manager became John W. Elliot, Wallsend-on-Tyne.
11.1931: Sold to Artaza y Compania, San Sebastian, Spain and renamed LOLITA.
1931: Renamed LOLITA A.
26.11.1934: Wrecked at Vieux Boucau, near Bayonne, whilst on a voyage from the Tyne to Pasajes with a cargo of coal.

Top: *Ruckinge* arriving Cardiff about 1936 *[Welsh Industrial and Maritime Museum, Ref: 469]*
Middle: *Stanlake*, completed as the *Marjorie S* in 1923. *[G.R.Scott collection]*
Bottom: *Murie S* lost in 1934 as the *Lolita A*. *[Nigel Farrell collection]*

Sheaf Field. [Nigel Farrell collection]

19. SHEAF FIELD
O.N. 148042 2,719g 1,682 320.3 x
42.9 x 24.3 feet
T. 3-cyl. by North Eastern Marine
Engineering Co. Ltd., Wallsend,
Newcastle-upon-Tyne; 323 NHP,
1,500IHP, 10½ knots.
25.6.1923: Launched by the Blyth
Shipbuilding and Dry Dock Co. Ltd.,
Blyth (Yard No. 225).
11.1923: Completed.
1.11.1923: Registered in the ownership
of the Sheaf Steam Shipping Co. Ltd.
(W.A. Souter and Co., managers),
Newcastle-upon-Tyne as SHEAF FIELD
28.10.1940: Mined two miles south west
of the Sunk Light Vessel whilst on a
voyage from the Tyne to London with a
cargo of coal.

29.10.1940: Beached 4½ miles from
Landguard Point and settled by the
stern. Beyond economical repair.
26.5.1941: Register closed.

20. SHEAF BROOK
O.N. 148069 2,179g 1344n 285.0 x
40.3 x 23.0 feet
T. 3-cyl. by MacColl and Pollock Ltd.,
Sunderland; 193 NHP, 1450IHP, 10.75
knots.
22.3.1924: Launched by the Blyth
Shipbuilding and Dry Dock Co. Ltd.,
Blyth (Yard No. 123).
6.1924: Completed.
6.6.1924: Registered in the ownership of
the Sheaf Steam Shipping Co. Ltd.
(W.A. Souter and Co., managers),
Newcastle-upon-Tyne as SHEAF
BROOK.

20.11.1935: Reported in distress in the
North Sea 110 miles east south east of
the Tyne in position 54.42 north by
01.30 east whilst on a voyage from the
Tyne to Hamburg with a cargo of coal.
1.1.1936: Posted missing.
4.12.1935: Register closed.

21. HALBEATH/PHILIPP M
O.N. 147908 2,085g 1,239n 274.5 x
39.9 x 23.3 feet
T. 3-cyl. by David Rowan and Co. Ltd.,
Glasgow; 220 NHP, 1,200 IHP, 10½
knots.
19.4.1924: Launched by the Burntisland
Shipbuilding Co. Ltd., Burntisland (Yard
No. 128).
25.6.1924: Registered in the ownership
of the Grahamston Shipping

Sheaf Brook. [G.R.Scott collection]

101

Halbeath on trials. *[Scottish Record Office GD313/13/20/1; Nigel Farrell collection]*

Co. Ltd. (T.L. Duff and Co., managers), Glasgow as HALBEATH.
21.9.1937: Sold to the Mooringwell Steamship Co. Ltd. (Frederick W. Moorsom, manager), Cardiff.
24.9.1937: Renamed PHILIPP M.
16.5.1942: Sold to the Hudson Steamship Co. Ltd., London.
24.2.1944: Torpedoed by a German E-boat two miles north of Hearty Knoll Buoy and sank in position 52.45 north by 02.12 east. She was on a voyage from the Tyne to London with 3,102 tons of coal in convoy FS 1371. Of 25 on board, seven were lost.
10.5.1944: Register closed.

22. TULLOCHMOOR/BRIGITTE/
EMPIRE SOAR/PREVEZA/
DANAPRIS/
ARMONIA/KEANYEW/CHARLIE
O.N. 148091 2,728g 1,686n 320.2 x 42.9 x 24.3 feet
T. 3-cyl. by North Eastern Marine Engineering Co. Ltd., Wallsend-on-Tyne; 323 NHP, 1,500 IHP, 10½ knots.
3.7.1924: Launched by the Blyth Shipbuilding and Dry Dock Co. Ltd., Blyth (Yard No. 229).
22.9.1924: Registered in the owner-ship of the Moor Line Ltd., Newcastle-upon-Tyne as TULLOCHMOOR.
10.1924: Completed.
6.1936: Sold to Franz L. Nimitz, Stettin,

Germany and renamed BRIGITTE.
5.1945: Captured by the Allies in Hamburg.
24.7.1945: Arrived at Methil.
27.8.1945: Registered in the owner-ship of the Ministry of War Transport, London (Sir Robert Ropner and Sons Ltd., Stockton-on-Tees, managers), as EMPIRE SOAR.
1946: Owners became the Ministry of Transport, London.
3.1947: Transferred to the Government of Greece, Athens and renamed PREVEZA.
1948: Sold to Synodinos Brothers, Piraeus, Greece and renamed DANAPRIS.

Tullochmoor of 1924. *[G.R.Scott collection]*

Left: *Danapris*, formerly the *Tullochmoor*, at Cardiff about 1950 with a deck cargo of pit props. *[Hansen 2998/3015, National Museums and Galleries of Wales]*

Middle: *Sheaf Crest* arriving at Hamburg. *[Hans Hartz, Nigel Farrell collection]*

Bottom: *Sheaf Crest* with a slight list - a frequent problem when carrying deck cargoes of timber. *[H.S.Appleyard collection]*

1957: Sold to A. Angelicoussis, D. Efthimiou and Co., Piraeus and renamed ARMONIA.
1959: Sold to Keanyew Shipping Co., Panama (Barreto Shipping and Trading Co. Ltd., Singapore) and renamed KEANYEW.
1960: Sold to Southern Commercial Co. Ltd., Panama and renamed CHARLIE.
30.1.1960: Arrived at Hong Kong to be broken up by Atlas Co. Ltd.

23. SHEAF CREST
O.N. 148097 2,730g 1,617 320.2 x 42.9 x 24.3 feet
T. 3-cyl. by North Eastern Marine Engineering Co. Ltd., Wallsend-on-Tyne; 305 NHP, 1500 NHP, 10½ knots.
31.7.1924: Launched by the Blyth Shipbuilding and Dry Dock Co. Ltd., Blyth (Yard No. 231).
10.1924: Completed.

16.10.1924: Registered in the ownership of the Sheaf Steam Shipping Co. Ltd. (W.A. Souter and Co., managers), Newcastle-upon-Tyne as SHEAF CREST
30.11.1939: Mined in position 51.32 north by 01.26 east whilst on a voyage from London to the Tyne in ballast.
7.12.1939: Register closed

24. USKMOOR/MARIANNE/ STENSNAES/BJARKE
O.N. 148108 2,729g 1,686n 320.2 x 42.9 x 24.3 feet
T. 3-cyl. by North Eastern Marine Engineering Co. Ltd., Wallsend-on-Tyne; 323 NHP, 1,500 IHP, 10½ knots.
30.9.1924: Launched by the Blyth Shipbuilding and Dry Dock Co. Ltd., Blyth (Yard No. 230).
3.12.1924: Registered in the ownership of the Moor Line Ltd., Newcastle-upon-Tyne as USKMOOR.
11.1924: Completed.
4.1936: Sold to Franz L. Nimtz, Stettin, Germany and renamed MARIANNE.
18.10.1946: Ownership transferred to the Danish Government, Copenhagen.

23.5.1947: Renamed STENSNAES.
10.1947: Sold to A/S Det Dansk-Norsk D/S (R. A. Robbert), Copenhagen and renamed BJARKE.
3.4.1948: Wrecked at Groningen, Kristiansandsfjord whilst on a voyage from Gdynia to Kristiansand with a cargo of coal.

25. CARLBEATH/MACBRAE/AYTON/ANGE/ALCYONE
O.N. 147934 2,117g 1,256n 274.5 x 39.9 x 23.3 feet
T. 3-cyl. by David Rowan and Co. Ltd., Glasgow.
14.10.1924: Launched by the Burntisland Shipbuilding Co. Ltd., Burntisland (Yard No. 132).
6.12.1924: Completed for the Grahamston Shipping Co. Ltd. (T.L. Duff and Co., managers), Glasgow as CARLBEATH.
1937: Sold to the Guardian Line Ltd. (Charles A. Roberts, manager), and renamed MACBRAE.
1941: Sold to the Hudson Steamship Co. Ltd., London.
1949: Sold to the J.B. Shipping Co. Ltd. (H.P. Marshall and Co. Ltd., managers), Middlesbrough and renamed AYTON.
1956: Sold to Compania Isla de Oro Ltda., San José, Costa Rica (Panaghis

G. Anghelatos, London) and renamed ANGE under the Panama flag.
1958: Sold to the Mediterranean Shipping Co. Inc., Panama (Casimiro Cosulich, Genoa, Italy, manager), and renamed ALCYONE.
24.8.1958: Stranded north east of Cape Sidheros, Crete after fire had broken out whilst on a voyage from Split to Aden with a cargo of cement. Abandoned by her crew.
25.8.1958: Fire extinguished.
28.8.1958: Refloated and towed to Piraeus.
Declared a constructive total loss.
1961: Sold for breaking up.

26. SHEAF WATER
O.N. 148115 2,730g 1,617n 320.2 x 42.9 x 24.3 feet
T. 3-cyl. by North Eastern Marine Engineering Co. Ltd., Newcastle-upon-Tyne; 323 NHP, 1,500 IHP, 10.5 knots.
28.10.1924: Launched by the Blyth Shipbuilding and Dry Dock Co. Ltd., Blyth (Yard No. 232).
1.1925: Completed.

16.1.1925: Registered in the ownership of the Sheaf Steam Shipping Co. Ltd. (W.A. Souter and Co., managers), Newcastle-upon-Tyne as SHEAF WATER.
7.10.1942: Torpedoed by the German E-boats S46, S79, S105 and S117 in position 53.06 north by 01.25 east off Cromer whilst on a voyage from London to Sunderland in ballast.
8.10.1942: Sank in position 52.48 north by 01.37 east whilst under tow.
29.4.1943: Register closed.

27. SAC 6°
2,472g 1,481n 297.2 x 43.1 x 23.5 feet
T. 3-cyl. by the North Eastern Marine Engineering Co. Ltd., Sunderland; 206 NHP.
19.7.1928: Launched by Swan, Hunter and Wigham Richardson Ltd., Sunderland (Yard No. 1353).
8.1928: Completed for Societa Anonima Cros, Barcelona, Spain as SAC 6°.
12.12.1938: Wrecked at St. Pierre, near Narbonne, France whilst on a voyage from Barcelona to Sete in ballast.

Top left: *Uskmoor. [Ivor Rooke collection]*
Above: *Carlbeath* on trials. *[Scottish Record Office GD313/13/23/1, Nigel Farrell collection]*
Bottom: *Ayton* of 1924. *[G.R. Scott collection]*

THE ABERDEEN ATLANTIC LINE
Peter Myers

The Aberdeen Atlantic Shipping Co. Ltd. was probably the shortest-lived of the many shipping firms which operated from Aberdeen in the nineteenth century. The firm was incorporated in 1895 and less than three years later it went into liquidation. Despite its brief existence, the company's principal claim to fame was that its three ocean steamships were the largest Aberdeen-owned vessels to have traded from their home port on a regular basis.

The Aberdeen Atlantic Line's short history was dominated by the tragic loss of its first ship, the *State of Georgia*, with the loss of all hands in the North Atlantic in 1896. Her fate was never established and it was speculated she had collided with an iceberg. The firm's brief existence was dogged by misfortune and demonstrated the struggles of operating a transatlantic livestock and cargo service with limited resources and elderly ships,

especially when ranged against the larger and well-established shipping lines.

The company's origins are closely linked with that of its managers, John Rust and Son, timber merchants and shipowners of Aberdeen. John Rust was an importer of foreign timber at Aberdeen and as the firm prospered his son, James, was taken into the company. After John Rust retired, James took over the running of the firm and by the 1880s the company had cornered 15% of the timber-importing trade at Aberdeen. The firm concentrated on North American timber and more than half of its supplies came from there, much of it imported into Aberdeen by its own sailing vessels.

In 1891, James Rust made the switch from sail to steam with the purchase of the iron, three-masted 2,490 gross ton steamship *State of Georgia* from the

The *State of Georgia* is seen at Larne about 1890, in her previous guise as an emigrant steamer. She is flying the houseflag of her owners, the State Line, whose departure point in Glasgow for its sailings to New York was Mavisbank Quay. After John Rust and Son bought her in 1893 she was converted at Aberdeen into a livestock and cargo carrier. *[Trustees of the National Museums and Galleries of Northern Ireland, negative no. W01/67/14]*

Allan Line. This former emigrant steamer had been built as the *Georgia* for the State Line of Glasgow in 1873 by the London and Glasgow Engineering and Iron Shipbuilding Co. Ltd. of Govan, Glasgow, a yard which was familiarly known as 'The Limited'. She was renamed *State of Georgia* for her owners' Glasgow-New York via Larne service. When the State Line went into liquidation in 1891, the Allan Line purchased the fleet of six ships and the goodwill of the company. The *State of Georgia* made only two round voyages for her new owners on the Glasgow-New York via Larne route before the 18-year-old steamer was bought by Rust.

The new acquisition, which cost £9,500, could do the work of Rust's four sailing ships and she also carried cargoes for other merchants. Her transatlantic service from Aberdeen to Montreal and Quebec operated under the informal title of the North of Scotland Line. Early during her new ownership in the spring of 1892 she ran aground while steaming down the St Lawrence River and had to return to port for repairs. As well as timber cargoes, the *State of Georgia* also carried considerable consignments of Canadian livestock, a trade which had begun to develop in the late 1880s and which during the following decade would involve major companies such as the Johnston Line and the consortium of Wilson and Furness Leyland Ltd. Apparently this new flood of cattle imports was not too disturbing for Scottish cattle-breeders since the foreign imports did not offer serious competition for the quality end of the market in which they specialised. At Aberdeen, these cattle imports were handled at Pocra Quay, which was within the tidal harbour.

A winter passage across the North Atlantic must have been a ghastly experience for the wretched animals and this is borne out by a winter voyage made by the *State of Georgia* in 1894. On 18th November, she left Montreal for Aberdeen via London, loaded with general cargo, 1,000 head of sheep and a large number of cattle. She had hardly cleared the Gulf of St Lawrence when she met the full force of a violent storm. Huge waves broke over the ship and both the first mate and a seaman were injured. Many cattle and sheep were washed overboard, and when she put back to Cape Breton Island for repairs, it was calculated that 29 cattle and 947 sheep had been lost.

Following repairs, the *State of Georgia* made a safe and uneventful passage to London. The final leg of the voyage, from the Thames to Aberdeen, was just as hazardous as her earlier experience in the Atlantic. She left London and once in the North Sea she met the full blast of a gale. The *State of Georgia* was driven off course as far as the Dogger Bank. In one violent pitch, she shipped water into the forecastle and even into the engine room. The winch on the forecastle was wrenched loose and washed overboard, ventilators snapped and went over the side, and the after cabin was rendered uninhabitable. The storm abated and the damaged *State of Georgia* reached Aberdeen without further mishap.

The rough winter passages had to be accepted as a matter of course and the only other noteworthy incident involving the *State of Georgia* occurred on 2nd June 1895, when she ran aground at the mouth of the Wester Burn, just north of Wick, Caithness, in dense fog. The Wick lifeboat was launched, but her services were declined since the steamer was refloated undamaged on the rising tide.

One of the primary reasons for the establishment of the Aberdeen Atlantic Shipping Co. Ltd. was to acquire the *State of Georgia* from John Rust and Son,

along with the goodwill of that firm's cargo trade between Aberdeen and North America. In the official contract, it was stated that the purchase of the steamship had been completed on 19th April 1895. However, in return for the allotment of 11,667 shares at 15 shillings per share (£8,750), John Rust and Son were required to hand over the ship on 8th August to the newly incorporated company. The vendor of the ship, James Rust, was appointed manager of the *State of Georgia* at an annual salary of £150, plus 7.5% of the net profits, and was expected to devote much of his "time, attention and abilities to the business of the Company".

The Aberdeen Atlantic Shipping Co. Ltd. was incorporated on 4th July 1895 with a nominal capital of £60,000 divided into 60,000 shares of £1 each. The company's registered office was at 146 Union Street, Aberdeen, but in November 1895 this was moved to 53 York Street, Footdee, Aberdeen, which was adjacent to Rust's timber yards and also to the shipbuilding yards of Hall, Russell and Co. Ltd. and Alexander Hall and Sons Ltd. Daniel Mearns, who was Lord Provost of Aberdeen, was appointed chairman of the board. Apart from being one of the pioneers of steam trawling at the port, he was heavily involved in the affairs of Aberdeen Harbour Board, which included such projects as the new fish market and the clearance of a dangerous reef which lay athwart the harbour's navigation channel.

With the aim of providing sailings at intervals of three weeks from Aberdeen to Montreal, and occasionally Quebec, a second steamship was needed and in 1896, the Aberdeen Atlantic Line purchased the iron, screw steamer 3,655 gross ton *Lord Gough* from the Lord Gough Steam Ship Co. Ltd. (Richardson, Spence and Co., managers). The *Lord Gough* had been built for G.M. Papayanni and Son, Liverpool by Laird Brothers, Birkenhead, and had an interesting history. Upon completion in April 1879, she was immediately chartered to the American Line of Liverpool and served on its Liverpool-Philadelphia service with the *Lord Clive* (3,386/1871). In 1885, her owners' title changed to the Lord Gough Steam Ship Co. Ltd. (G.M. Papayanni and Son, managers) and three years later the *Lord Gough* was sold to the American Line (now owned by the International Navigation Company, Philadelphia), but still registered at Liverpool. She remained with the American Line until 1892 when she passed to Richardson, Spence and Co., Liverpool.

An advertisement for the Aberdeen Atlantic Line's stated that sailings would be at intervals of three weeks between Aberdeen and Montreal/Quebec, from the middle of April to the middle of November. During the winter, when the St. Lawrence was frozen over, the Canadian terminus was St. John, New Brunswick. Other British ports-of-call included Newcastle and Leith.

Soon after her acquisition by the Aberdeen Atlantic Line, the *State of Georgia* was taken in hand by Hall, Russell's yard and modifications were made to make her more suitable for the flourishing North American cattle trade. The refit included the removal of all passenger cabins and some of the cabin skylights. Two gangways were cut in the ship's sides, one on each side, so as to facilitate the loading and unloading of livestock. In contemporary press reports the *State of Georgia* was described as having a black funnel with red over white over blue bands.

During 1896, the *State of Georgia* made five voyages from Montreal and Quebec, loaded with general cargo and livestock. The difficulty of finding cargoes at Aberdeen for Canada would suggest why she left Aberdeen on 7th October 1896 with 84 tons of general cargo for New Fairwater (Danzig) where she loaded 1,808 tons of bagged sugar for Montreal. A further large consignment awaited her at the German port when she left Aberdeen for the last time on 9th December 1896.

The *State of Georgia* was commanded by Captain John Stewart, who had previously been master of Rust's barque *Lumberman's Lassie* (979/1870). Captain Stewart had succeeded Captain Robert Crombie as master of the *State of Georgia,* with the latter transferring to the *Lord Gough*. Under his command, Captain Stewart had a crew of 31, of whom 24 came from Aberdeen, six from Newburgh, Aberdeenshire, one from Liverpool, while the carpenter was signed on at New Fairwater. At the Baltic port, the *State of Georgia* loaded 1,912 tons of sugar in bags which, with 600 tons of bunker coal, raised her deadweight tonnage to 2,512 tons and gave her the required winter freeboard. She sailed on 23rd December and on the morning of the 28th she signalled 'All well' to Dunnet Head Lighthouse, which stands sentinel over the Pentland Firth. After leaving the firth, she headed out into the North Atlantic. She was never seen again.

It was when she became a fortnight overdue at Halifax, Nova Scotia, that the first anxieties came to be expressed. James Rust was in regular contact with Halifax and New York, but still no news came of the overdue ship. The worries intensified when steamships on passage from Europe to St. John, New Brunswick, reported numerous icebergs, and more than one ship entered port with collision damage after coming into contact with icebergs. When she was 16 days overdue, an approach was made to the Admiralty requesting it to make a search for her, but unfortunately this was turned down. At the end of January 1897, informed opinion at Halifax believed that the *State of Georgia* was already lost, probably caught in the icebergs to the north of Nova Scotia where immense fields of ice were drifting about. The Hamburg-Amerika cargo steamer *Adria* (5,458/1896) arrived at Philadelphia from New Fairwater two days overdue, and although she had traversed the same route as the *State of Georgia*, had failed to see anything of her.

With both the Admiralty and the Canadian Government refusing to send search vessels, James Rust took matters into his own hands and chartered the sealing steamer *Nimrod*, which left St. John's, Newfoundland, for a six-day search among the ice floes, 100 miles north of St. John's. Her search proved fruitless, and no remaining traces of the *State of Georgia* and her crew were found. The *Nimrod* was to achieve her niche in the history of polar exploration just 10 years later, when, in 1907, she carried Lieutenant Ernest Shackleton's expedition to the Antarctic on what was to be an almost successful attempt to reach the South Pole.

Since they were running a cargo-liner service, the Aberdeen Atlantic Line's directors made every effort to charter a suitable steamship to replace their loss since there was 3,000 tons of cargo waiting at Halifax to be loaded for Aberdeen and Leith. Their efforts were in vain, resulting in the *Lord Gough* having to make a return voyage from New York to Newcastle-on-Tyne, discharge her cargo there and sail to Halifax to load the large cargo consignment intended for the *State of Georgia*.

Thirteen days after leaving the Tyne, the *Lord Gough* encountered hurricane-force gales, the like of which had never been experienced by her master, Captain Robert Crombie, who had served at sea since boyhood. The continual exposure to such severe weather told upon Captain Crombie's health, and he suffered an attack of influenza which led to a severe bronchial

The *Lord Gough* was originally a transAtlantic emigrant ship and she is shown wearing the funnel colours used by the American Line between 1884 and 1892. She started her last voyage from Liverpool to Philadelphia on 9th February 1895, and was acquired the following year by the Aberdeen Atlantic Line and converted to cargo carrying. *[Author's collection]*

Hankow in the Thames. *[National Maritime Museum, Peter Newall collection]*

infection. On the return passage to Leith, Captain Crombie had become very ill and the *Lord Gough* put into Aberdeen Bay where her master could be put ashore. Sadly, Captain Crombie died aboard his ship on 15th April 1897, aged only 51.

It was a bitter blow to the company's directors to have lost the *State of Georgia* and then to lose an experienced master like Captain Crombie in the space of a couple of months. In the late 1890s, marine casualties in the North Atlantic were quite appalling. During the winter of 1898-99, there was a distressing catalogue of ships posted missing and never heard of again. Exactly two years after the *State of Georgia* passed Dunnet Head, the steamer *Almida* (2,498/1886), recently ex-*Cedar Branch*, outbound from the Tyne, passed the northerly headland on 21st December 1898 and then disappeared with all hands.

A Court of Inquiry into the disappearance of the *State of Georgia* was held at Aberdeen Sheriff Court in April 1897. After carefully examining the available evidence, the court was satisfied the ship was seaworthy, that previous defects in the boilers and furnaces had been satisfactorily repaired and that the ship was properly and efficiently manned when she made her last voyage. As to the cause of her disappearance, the court could offer no definite answer. A number of theories had been advanced, including the possibility of a collision with a derelict or with ice, or struck rocks in a fog, or foundered through stress of weather. The latter theory was partly discounted because the *State of Georgia* was a strong, well-found ship, which had weathered worse conditions in previous voyages across the Atlantic.

Despite their tragic loss, the company's directors decided to maintain their transatlantic service by purchasing a replacement steamship. By May 1897, their new acquisition, the *Hankow* was loading at Montreal for Aberdeen. Like the *State of Georgia* and the *Lord Gough*, the *Hankow* was a former passenger and cargo ship and had been built by Charles Mitchell and Co., Low Walker-on-Tyne, in 1873 for E.H. Watts and Co. (later Watts, Milburn and Co.), London. She measured 3,594

gross tons and had a deadweight tonnage of 5,000 tons. Propulsion was by a two-cylinder compound steam engine of 1,320 IHP, which gave her a service speed of 10 knots. The *Hankow* and her sister-ship *Whampoa* were notable as being among the first passenger liners to have their saloons extending across the deck from side to side. Both ships participated in the Australian trade while the *Hankow* was chartered frequently by the Government for trooping, notably during the first Boer War of 1881. By that date, ownership had been transferred to W. Milburn and Co., London, who sold her to the Aberdeen Atlantic Line in 1897. The *Hankow* was probably the only ship built by Charles Mitchell to be registered at Aberdeen, which was his birthplace and where he had served his early apprenticeship as an engineer.

In October 1897, the moving spirit behind the Aberdeen Atlantic Line, James Rust, died suddenly at the age of 49. The loss of the *State of Georgia* must have been a severe, personal blow to him and one can only surmise that the anxieties of running a transatlantic cargo-liner service with limited financial resources and against the stiff opposition from the larger and more powerful shipping lines, must have told against his health. His son, John Rust, took over the position of interim manager and secretary. A few weeks after the death of James Rust, the *Hankow* arrived at Greenock on 3rd November for lay-up, while a month later the *Lord Gough*, under the command of Captain Ninnes, completed the last commercial voyage made by an Aberdeen Atlantic ship when she arrived at Aberdeen on 30th December from Montreal via the Tyne.

The suspension of all future sailings for the company's two ships was the first hint that all was not well. The firm's true financial plight was made public at an extraordinary meeting of the company on 31st January 1898, when it was confirmed that the Aberdeen Atlantic Shipping Co. Ltd. was to be voluntarily wound up on 13th February and that a liquidator was to be appointed. The complete winding-up of the company proved to be a lengthy affair and was not completed until 6th November 1901.

The two steamships were sold. The *Hankow* was bought by Wilh. Wilhelmsen, of Tonsberg, Norway in 1898 and renamed *Dunnet,* which seems a rather ironic choice of name since it was from Dunnet Head that the ill-fated *State of Georgia* was last seen. Sadly, the *Dunnet* suffered a similar fate to the Aberdeen steamer. On 6th April 1899, she sailed from Barry, bound for Genoa, and subsequently disappeared. It was believed that she had foundered in the Bay of Biscay. The *Lord Gough* was sold in 1898 to G. Tardy, Italy and in July that year was re-sold for breaking-up at Genoa.

The managing firm of John Rust and Son owned no more ships but continued trading as timber merchants at Aberdeen until it was taken over by George Gordon and Co. in 1926. The Aberdeen Atlantic Line ought to be seen as a brave attempt to provide a locally controlled ocean link with Canada. The Thomson Line of Dundee already provided such a service, and this continued after 1907 when that company was acquired by Cairns, Noble and Co., of Newcastle-on-Tyne.

During the twentieth century, Ellerman's Wilson Line traded between Aberdeen and Montreal/Quebec right up until 1966, with Canadian flour being the principal import cargo. The Hull-based company was succeeded briefly by G. Heyn's Head Line and it was left to that firm's *Ramore Head* (6,195/1948) to terminate Aberdeen's sea trade with Canada when she arrived at the port on 19th February 1967.

Fleet list

1. STATE OF GEORGIA 1891-1896 Iron
O.N. 68047 2,489g 1,507n 330.3 x 36.3 x 21.2 feet
C. 2-cyl. by the London and Glasgow Engineering and Iron Shipbuilding Co. Ltd., Govan; 400 NHP.
6.1873: Launched by the London and Glasgow Engineering and Iron Shipbuilding Co. Ltd., Govan for George W. Clark, trading as the State Line Steamship Co. Ltd., Glasgow as GEORGIA.
1874: Renamed STATE OF GEORGIA.
1876: Owner became the State Steam Ship Co. Ltd., Glasgow.

1891: Sold to J. and A. Allan, Glasgow.
1891: Acquired by James Rust, Aberdeen.
1895: Owner became the Aberdeen Atlantic Shipping Co. Ltd. (John Rust and Son, managers), Aberdeen.
23.12.1896: Left New Fairwater (Danzig) for Halifax, Nova Scotia with general cargo and disappeared after passing Dunnet Head on 28.12.1896.

2. LORD GOUGH 1896-1898 Iron
O.N. 81266 3,397g 2,159n 382.8 x 40.2 x 30.0 feet
C. 2-cyl. by Laird Brothers, Birkenhead; 450 NHP
11.1878: Launched by Laird Brothers, Birkenhead (Yard No. 447).
4.1879: Completed for George M. Papayanni and Son, Liverpool as LORD GOUGH.
1882: Owner became the Lord Gough Steam Ship Co. Ltd. (G.M. Papayanni and Son, managers), Liverpool.
1888: Sold to the American Line (now owned by the International Navigation Company, Philadelphia), but still registered at Liverpool.*
1892: Owner became the Lord Gough Steam Ship Co. Ltd. (Richardson, Spence and Co., managers), Liverpool.
1896: Acquired by the Aberdeen Atlantic Shipping Co. Ltd. (John Rust and Son, managers), Aberdeen.
7.1898: Sold to G. Tardy for breaking up at Genoa.

* This may have been a charter rather than a sale, as contemporary issues of the Mercantile Navy List, but not Lloyd's Register, record her as continuing under the ownership of Papayanni's single-ship company.

3. HANKOW 1897-1898 Iron
O.N. 68510 3,594g 2,332n 389.0 x 42.1 x 28.8 feet
C. 2-cyl. by R. and W. Hawthorn, Newcastle-upon-Tyne; 500 NHP, 1,320 IHP, 10 knots.
7.10.1873: Launched by Charles Mitchell and Co. Low Walker, Newcastle-upon-Tyne (Yard No. 290).
21.2.1874: Completed for Edmund H. Watts, London as HANKOW.
7.1879: Owners became William Milburn and Co., London.
5.1897: Acquired by the Aberdeen Atlantic Shipping Co. Ltd. (John Rust and Son, managers), Aberdeen.
1898: Sold to Wilh. Wilhelmsen, Tonsberg, Norway and renamed DUNNET.
6.4.1899: Left Barry for Genoa with a cargo of coal and disappeared.

SOURCES AND ACKNOWLEDGEMENTS

We thank all who gave permission for their photographs to be used, and for help in finding photographs we are particularly grateful to Tony Smith, Jim McFaul and David Whiteside of the World Ship Photo Library; to Ian Farquhar, F.W. Hawks, Peter Newall, Ivor Rooke, William Schell, George Scott; and to David Hodge and Bob Todd of the National Maritime Museum, and other museums and institutions listed.

Research sources have included the *Registers* of William Schell and Tony Starke, *Lloyd's Register, Lloyd's Confidential Index, Lloyd's War Losses, Mercantile Navy Lists, Marine News* and *Shipbuilding and Shipping Record.* Use of the facilities of the World Ship Society's Central Record, the Guildhall Library, the Public Record Office and Lloyd's Register of Shipping are gratefully acknowledged, and Dr Malcolm Cooper is thanked for checking Second World War losses. Particular thanks also to Heather Fenton for editorial and indexing work, and Marion Clarkson for accountancy services.

THE LAST YEARS OF THE LOCH LINE
The surviving voyage results for the Loch Line are held in the small Aitken, Lilburn and Co. collection in the Mitchell Library in Glasgow. The fleet lists have been compiled from the closed registers in the National Archives at Kew (classes BT 108 and BT 110). Supplementary material on crews and masters has come from the National Archives' sample of Crew Agreements (BT 99) and from the Lloyd's Captains Registers. Some background

material has been taken from Basil Lubbock's 'The Colonial Clippers' and 'The Last of the Windjammers'. The author has also drawn on unpublished work by David Burrell and James H. Barr and has benefited from valuable commentary from Howard Dick and Tom Stevens. Dr John Naylon is thanked for supplying most of the photographs for this feature.

THE BLUE FUNNEL TRANSPACIFIC SERVICE
All photographs are by courtesy of the Puget Sound Maritime Historical Society, P.O. Bix 97321, Seattle, WA98109, USA.

THE ABERDEEN ATLANTIC LINE
Reference to the *Almida* disappearing is in Nelson V.H., 'A Fateful Year' *Sea Breezes,* August 1948 page 122.

THE STAINBURN INCIDENT
Photographs on page 111 and lower page 113 are by Richard Brothers, Penzance and are held by the Morrab Library, Penzance. All others are from the Pawlyn/Holman Collection and are now held by the Royal Institution of Cornwall, River Street, Truro.

STAINBURN STEAMSHIP Co. Ltd.: A BRIEF HISTORY
The company and its history were researched by Roy Fenton largely from material at the National Archives, Kew, including the company's file, in class BT31, and closed registers in class BT110.

THE STAINBURN INCIDENT
Tony Pawlyn

In March 1906, N. Holman and Sons of Penzance were called upon to execute urgent damage repairs to the Workington steam collier *Stainburn,* which had survived a close encounter with the Runnelstone Reef. Although long established as iron and brass founders, and well renowned throughout Cornwall as mining and agricultural engineers, this little family firm had only recently acquired outright ownership of the Penzance Dry Dock. For many years their main centre of activity had been the St. Just mining area, served by their Tregaseal Foundry. In more recent years this had been supplemented by a Penzance branch with the acquisition of the Borough Arms Foundry. More recently still, with the great expansion of iron and steel shipping employed in the coastal trades, they had augmented their extensive foundry business with increasing ship repair work. For well over a decade Holmans had carried out ship repair work on a sub-contractual basis for the Penzance Dry Dock, Coal and Trading Company. But, during 1904-5, when the latter hit hard times, the dry dock and premises were advantageously snapped up by the Holmans.

The actual repair of the *Stainburn* was not a major job in itself, but the challenge of quickly and efficiently returning the damaged steamer to full seaworthiness was seen by the directors as a stepping stone to future work. This job would get them noticed in north western quarters, and the potential prestige was sufficient to cause Percy Holman (a partner and keen photographer), to record this operation. His photographs provide an interesting series, and as Cornish mining declined, ship repair work became their core business, and the repairs to the *Stainburn* helped establish their reputation for good workmanship, effectively and efficiently executed.

Rock dodgers

During the era of steam coasters, deep water seamen and longshoremen alike somewhat disparagingly referred to those employed in that trade as 'mud-hoppers' or 'rock dodgers.' This arose from their tendency to follow simple straight line courses from promontory to headland, from beacon to buoy. Accurate navigation by calculation was not their strong point. By familiarity and rote they came to know the coastal waters like the backs of their hands - or so they thought. Few enough carried more than some old large scale charts, others carried old school atlases, but the majority relied mainly on their memory and occasional notebooks to recall sea and land marks and the standard courses and distances between them. Inevitably there were many accidents - sheer numbers ensured this. The major ones resulted in the total loss of ships and lives, but the minor ones provided steady work for salvage and ship repair companies all round the coast.

The Penzance Dry Dock was situated conveniently near the Land's End and the notorious Runnelstone Reef. Accordingly a steady flow of repair work came to the dry dock, following its construction by John Mathews in 1810 as '...a safe and very commodious DRY DOCK, capable of receiving Ships or Vessels from One Hundred to Five Hundred Tons burthen...'. Nearly a century later, when the new Wharf Road was extended to provide a direct road link between the commercial heart of the port, the railway station and all points east of Penzance, the dry dock had been totally rebuilt and realigned on the line of the old shipbuilding slip. Previously everything carried by land in or out of the town had to be conveyed through the middle of the town, up and down a steep hill, and along narrow twisting streets. The new Wharf Road alleviated all that, but cut off the old dry dock basin from the sea. The lack of free space directly inland of the dry dock prevented its extension in that direction, but realigning it parallel to the new road enabled them to build a bigger dock. Access to the dock was now via the Abbey Basin, where vessels had to be turned through 90 degrees to enter the dry dock. The Abbey Basin was also practically isolated by the construction of the new Wharf Road, but this section of the road had been built as a viaduct, with a swing bridge giving access to and from the main harbour.

A glancing blow

At the time of the incident, February 1906, the Workington coastal steamer *Stainburn* was on a voyage from Llanelly to Great Yarmouth. She was barely two years old, having been completed at Workington by R. Williamson and Son early in 1904, and was under the command of Captain Thomas Little, her only master since her completion. Laden with 400 tons of coals, her passage down the Bristol Channel had passed without incident, until just after midday on Tuesday 27th February, when she rounded the Land's End to shape up for her run up the English Channel. We do not know who had the watch at the time and it may be that, clearing the Land's End just after noon, the master and some hands were below having their midday meal.

Whatever, the weather was fine and visibility was good. There was a light breeze from the north west with a bit of a swell rolling in from the south'ard - almost ideal conditions. However, as she approached the Runnelstone buoy it would appear that whoever had the wheel tried to cut the corner by bearing up for the Lizard too soon. It had been done many times before by many vessels, and would be tried many times again, but on this occasion luck was not with them.

Pushing on at 'full ahead' and making about ten knots, at close on dead low water the steamer fell into the hollow of a swell and struck a glancing blow on one of the outer guards of the Runnelstone Reef. It was about 13.00 when she struck. The grinding shriek of the hull plates tearing on the rocks and the staggering lurch of the little steamer left no one in doubt of what had happened. By good fortune the lifting surge of the following swell and her own momentum immediately carried the *Stainburn* clear. For a moment all was confusion on board, but a hurried check revealed that she was making water in the engine room, although they could not locate the actual point of damage.

Unable to see how much damage had been sustained, or precisely where it has occurred, it was quickly apparent to Captain Little and his crew that the influx of water was more than her pumps could handle. Accordingly he headed up into Mount's Bay, all the time looking for a suitable place to beach her. Wisely he rejected Porthcurno, where grounding on a rising tide would almost inevitably have resulted in the total loss of his command. Although there seemed no immediate danger of foundering, Captain Little was taking no unnecessary risks, and first ordered the boats swung out as a precaution. He then had an inverted ensign hoisted as a signal for assistance. Their situation was far from desperate, but there was considerable anxiety on board as they steamed along the rock bound coast under the 'western land' with no apparent haven in sight..

Initially she was able to maintain her best speed of about 10 knots, but as the *Stainburn* ran up into Mount's Bay she was settling perceptibly deeper in the water. In the engine room the water level rose steadily but surely, until it was about waist deep over the engine room deck plates. At this stage the rising sea water flooded the boiler furnaces, extinguishing the fires and cutting off her only power source. She was somewhere off Lamorna Cove when her fires were extinguished, and her residual steam pressure began to fall off causing the little steamer to gradually lose way.

Her ensign flying upside down

In the tiny pilot lookout at Penzance a long glass was almost permanently focused on the low dark silhouette of St. Clement's Island, just off Mousehole. It was from here that much of their pilotage business first came into sight, as indeed did the sinking *Stainburn*. The distressed steamer was first seen off the island a little after 13.30 by the Penzance pilots. She was then barely making headway, well down by the stern and wallowing perceptibly. In addition to her alarming trim, the sight of her ensign flying upside down called attention to her plight, and pilots Alfred Vingoe and George Trewhella, assisted by their boatman Joseph Hill, immediately put off to her aid in their pilot boat. As this was a modest harbour gig, not one of the fleet 32-footers with their six-man rowing crews, it took some time for them to pull across the bay. Thus it was about 14.00 when they reached the stricken steamer. She was now mid way between St. Clement's Island and the Low Lee buoy, having barely covered one mile in the last half hour. The tide was now about one hour's flood, and the southerly swell rolling in was more pronounced in the shallow head-waters of the bay.

When pilot Alfred Vingoe boarded her, she was still just under way, and he was soon informed that the *Stainburn* had struck the Runnelstone. She had been making water steadily ever since, with her pumps unable to clear the inrush. It was not revealed whether her steam pumps were still on line, but it must have been an agonising decision whether to save all the residual steam they could for the engines, or to continue trying to work the pumps. Her lifeboats, lowered to deck level, were within inches of the water, and she was clearly close to sinking. But just how close no one knew. Nobody on board was able to make the critical buoyancy calculations and, in addition to her flooded engine room, there was now over a foot of water in her main hold. Quite how long the engine room bulkhead would last, no one knew - though she was still a relatively new vessel.

Pilot Vingoe found Captain Little almost beside himself with anxiety, and in his later evidence he stated that her master seemed to him to be 'flabbergasted and excited,' requesting him 'to get his ship into a port of safety', but by this time there was very little residual steam left in her boiler.

Hoisting two buckets

Unable to make more than a hurried assessment of their imminent danger Vingoe, not wishing to risk taking the swell beam-on with so much free water in her, decided to make for Newlyn. Penzance, with its ship repair facilities might have been a better choice, but Newlyn was much closer - now less than three-quarters of a mile away - and the risk of her capsizing was a very material one. Hoisting two buckets (there being no black balls available) as a signal that the *Stainburn* was not under command, Vingoe held the best course he could for Newlyn harbour mouth, ghosting in with the swell and tide, and a whisper of steam.

At Newlyn the spring mackerel fishery was getting into full swing, and a large number of fishing boats - Mount's Bay luggers, Lowestoft smacks, together with Lowestoft and Yarmouth steam drifters - were in the harbour, anchored off, or entering or leaving. Approaching Newlyn with almost imperceptible steerage way *Stainburn* became virtually unmanageable. And as Vingoe tried to con the *Stainburn* through the milling fishing craft she nearly sunk a 'bummer's gig' as she gave it a glancing blow, fortuitously avoiding a steam drifter that shot across her bows.

Half tide, on a hazy afternoon, looking out through the 'gaps' at Newlyn. Mount's Bay luggers and craft from Lowestoft, Yarmouth and Plymouth congregate near the harbour mouth before a night's fishing. Taken during the era of our story, this shot includes a number of the new breed of steam drifters, with their 'Woodbine' funnels. The *Stainburn* grounded roughly where the Plymouth smack rides, and a bummer's gig, like the one she nearly ran down, heads in for the South Pier on the right. *[Richards Brothers/ Morrab Library, Penzance]*

Her lame approach to Newlyn had been observed by many people, a number of whom had gathered on the quay heads. These included Newlyn Harbour Master (William Oats Strick), and the Chief Officer of Coastguards (Charles Runnalls). The former was most anxious lest the stricken steamer should sink in his harbour mouth and become a major obstruction during this busy fishing season - the spring mackerel fishing providing the harbour's main revenue . The latter had been alerted by the Coastguards at Mousehole, having observed as the steamer passed by that her ensign was hoisted upside down and a crewman was seen rushing about her deck brandishing an axe. Sufficiently alarmed by this report, Runnalls turned out a party of his men fully armed - just in case there was trouble on board. It was after all only six years since the Newlyn riots, when the local fishermen had risen against the visiting Lowestoft and Yarmouth fishermen. Ostensibly the reason was for fishing on Sundays, but in reality it was because they worked seven days a week without a break, leaving no respite for the inland fish markets to recover. Chief Officer Runnalls' fears on this occasion were, however, groundless - there was no mutiny on board.

Aground in the harbour mouth

When the *Stainburn* left Llanelly the previous day she drew 10 feet of water forward, and 12 feet aft. She now drew about 13 feet 6 inches aft. This may not seem a great increase, but bearing in mind that she had a nominal freeboard of just nine inches amidships when loaded down to her marks, it was a significant increase. As she entered the 'gaps' between the two pier heads she took the bottom and came fast aground in the harbour mouth, some 20 to 30 feet off the south pier. In this situation she left no room for other vessels to pass between her and the South, or Lighthouse Pier. There was a wider gap of 100 feet between her and the knuckle of the 'Victoria', or North Pier, but even so she was a major obstruction in a hazardous situation. It was a little after 14.30 when she grounded, and shortly afterwards, having assured himself that his command was in no immediate danger, Captain Little went ashore to telegraph his owners. It was essential in his mind that he appraised the owners of his current situation and sought their advice and instructions.

It was about this time that the first telegram reporting the incident was sent off to Lloyd's of London - 'Penzance, Feb. 27, 3.33 p.m. - STAINBURN (s) - of Workington - from Llanelly for Yarmouth - cargo coals - put into Newlyn this afternoon having struck Runnelstone - Engine room full water - supposed holed under engine room.'

Meanwhile, Vingoe took stock and reconsidered the options. Lying aground in the fairway, the *Stainburn* was a hazard to other shipping, especially as the practice was for vessels entering Newlyn harbour to keep to port. No doubt the harbour master was also bringing pressure to bear to get her removed. At first Vingoe thought she could be warped ahead as the tide made. This was attempted, but there was insufficient steam pressure to drive her windlass effectively, and she then appeared to be filling as fast as the tide made, keeping her tight fast on the bed of the harbour. (In his evidence Vingoe called it a capstan rather than a windlass, but this seems unlikely on a steam coaster, though some did have capstans aft.)

Towards the middle of the afternoon there were a number of Lowestoft steam drifters getting ready for sea for a night's fishing. Their increasing activity naturally took Vingoe's attention. If he could only get her afloat again, there was a good chance that one of these could tow her across to Penzance. Also, with the increasing depth of water on the rising tide, it was now apparent that the swell that had first influenced him to make for Newlyn had lessened appreciably. Her bows remained well afloat, and it was clear that only a short section of the heel of her keel was actually aground.

Uneasy with the disappearance of her master ashore, which prevented Vingoe from taking any immediate further action, he now blew her whistle to recall him - so there was still some steam left. On Captain Little's return Vingoe advised him that it was dangerous to remain where they were. But, when he suggested that they should now take his steamer over to Penzance, Captain Little questioned how this could be achieved, when they had barely got her into Newlyn such a short while ago.

New steam drifters

Vingoe (probably having already sounded out her skipper), now pointed out one of the new steam drifters, the *Ludham Castle*. She had a good head of steam up and was in the final stages of preparing for sea. He suggested that her skipper, or one of the others, might be prepared to give them a tow, and Little agreed to give this a try. Skipper George Bishop was given a hail, and he undertook to try and tow them off and haul them over to Penzance. Two Newlyn pilots (Richard Pollard, senior and junior) and their boatman (George Glasson), leant a hand in passing a tow rope between the drifter and the steamer. Then, after taking up the slack, skipper Bishop called down for full power, and the *Ludham Castle* surged against the taught tow line. Despite the rising tide, there was a long anxious period before the drifter's engine driving at full power was able to start the *Stainburn* moving. Once moving however, she was quickly dragged off stern first into deeper water, arcing clear of the pier head.

Clearing Newlyn shortly after 16.00 they shifted the tow line to the steamer's bows, and set off for Penzance. This entailed taking a dog-leg course to the southward to clear the reef of rocks running out to the Gear Pole - then exhibiting a day mark consisting of a wrought iron pole surmounted by a spherical wrought iron cage, forged by Holman & Sons some years previously. During the course of this short voyage someone ashore (presumably the Lloyd's Agent) fired off another telegram to Lloyd's - 'Penzance, Feb. 27, 4.40 p.m. - STAINBURN - this steamer is now towing from Newlyn Harbour to Penzance.'

As they made a sweeping turn to round the Gear Pole, the tow rope parted, leaving the steamer wallowing ominously for some time before the connection could be re-established. Despite renewed fears of imminent foundering, the tow was eventually reconnected, and the stricken steamer was hauled safely into Penzance harbour.

Fortunately, after her somewhat protracted tow, she now only drew six inches more water than when she left Newlyn. Now drawing 14 feet aft, she seemed to have attained a degree of near equilibrium before she again took the ground inside Penzance harbour. When later questioned Vingoe was not sure what time they arrived in Penzance. High water that evening was around 20.00, but having had considerable difficulty in getting her into a secure berth alongside the eastern wall of the dock, it was 20.30 that evening before they had squared away for the night. Even then her stem was stuck in the mud some way off the quayside.

Docking the *Stainburn*

Over the next few days a series of brief progress reports appeared in the columns of 'Lloyd's List':
'Penzance, Feb. 28 - At low water today the master of the steamer STAINBURN tried to locate the damage, but, there being two or three feet of water round her, and the vessel flat at the bottom, he was unsuccessful. The owner of the STAINBURN thinks that it will be necessary to discharge her for examination. It is believed that the cargo is dry, and the water confined to the engine room.

Penzance March 2 - It has been decided to discharge and store the steamer STAINBURN's cargo and re-load same when vessel has been repaired. The discharge has commenced, and it is expected that she will be ready to proceed from March 12 to 15th. The leak has been found and is being temporarily stopped.

Penzance March 3 - It has not yet been possible to get at the damage to the steamer STAINBURN's bottom. A steam pump has been engaged, as the hand pump has failed to keep the water from the engine room.

Penzance March 6 - The steam pump now on board the steamer STAINBURN can easily keep the water under control. She will probably dry dock March 8.

Penzance March 10 - The steamer STAINBURN was dry-docked yesterday afternoon and found to be damaged in three places, the principal hole being about 10 inches by 2. She is expected to be out of dry dock about March 21.

Penzance Mar. 24 - The steamer STAINBURN came out of dry dock this afternoon after completing repairs. She will reship the discharged cargo March 26 and probably proceed for Yarmouth on the 27th.'

While these reports set out the bald course of events, they mask the sheer hard work entailed. First her cargo of coal had to be discharged. While one or two of the regular coal merchants had mobile grab cranes, these were not usually available for hire. Coal discharged from the schooners, with their small hatches, and other craft was still being 'jumped' out of the hold, and conveyed ashore on the backs of stevedores, running the plank. On the quayside it was dumped into waiting horse-drawn carts and whisked away to storage cellars. Jumping out 400 tons took a couple of days. But despite this lightening, her stern remained fast on the bottom, while her engine room flooded with every tide.

Above: Alongside the eastern wall of the 'floating' dock, discharging coal from the *Stainburn* over three precarious planks. Nothing at first appears to be amiss, but her stern lying so far off the quayside tells us she is well aground. *[Pawlyn/Holman Collection/Royal Institution of Cornwall, Truro.]*

Below: Discharging coal from the steamer *Oakford* at Penzance. Despite the crack in the original glass plate negative, this shot conveys all the movement, hustle and bustle, as well as the all pervading dirt and grime, associated with discharging coal at a small port. *[Richards Brothers/Morrab Library, Penzance]*

Getting her afloat, if only for a short while, was the next key move. But, throughout these operations, 'reasonable economy' would have been the watchword governing all their efforts. Manual labour was relatively cheap, but hand pumps proved unable to overcome the influx of water, no matter how much effort was applied. Eventually those concerned were forced to hire a steam salvage pump (or pumps) to do the job.

Meanwhile, as her discharge progressed, arrangements were made with N. Holman & Sons to have the *Stainburn* dry docked for a survey. The dock appears to have been occupied, though it is not known by what vessel, but this was a heaven sent opportunity for N. Holman & Sons, and one that could not be turned away. Eventually all the conditions were right, but it was still eleven days after her encounter with the Runnelstone before she could be docked.

The main problem lay in getting the little steamer sufficiently buoyant to clear the dock sill and onto the keel blocks. The availability of steam salvage pumps would not normally have been a problem at Penzance, where two renowned salvage companies were normally based - the Cornish Salvage Company and the Western Marine Salvage Company. But their vessels, the *Etna, Zephyr, Greencastle,* and *Lady of the Isles* were all at sea on jobs. Fortunately the steam barge *Jumbo,* of Cardiff, was then employed in dredging operations at Newlyn, and she was duly hired to provide the essential auxiliary steam power. This proved effective, and the salvage pumps were soon discharging a steady stream of water from the bowels of the *Stainburn,* which raised her sufficiently to manoeuvre her into a new more secure berth. Even then it was another four days before the dry dock was available, the tides were right, and everyone involved was satisfied that she could be docked without significant risk to vessel or dry dock.

Docking the *Stainburn* included the tricky task of negotiating the break in the new Wharf Road, created by the Ross Bridge, a swing bridge of distinctly railway turntable appearance, but in fact specifically made for this location. Jacked up hydraulically, the bridge had to be swung aside manually to open the way for shipping. This tricky task was accomplished towards the top end of a rising tide on the afternoon of Friday 9th March and the *Stainburn* was successfully manoeuvred into the dry dock with inches to spare.

Opposite top: Lying off the north wall of the dock, the heavy pall of smoke from the *Jumbo* and a steady stream of water from the scuppers, tells us that the salvage pumps are fully at work pumping out the *Stainburn.* Alongside the dock wall lies the local mineral schooner *Golden Light,* built at Truro in 1864. She arrived from Cardiff with coal on 5th March, and sailed again for Newport about 10 days later. *[Pawlyn/Holman Collection/Royal Institution of Cornwall, Truro.]*

Opposite bottom: Ross Bridge has swung aside. Horse-drawn traffic is forced to wait while spectators gawk as the *Jumbo* assists the *Stainburn* into the Abbey turning basin. *[Pawlyn/Holman Collection/Royal Institution of Cornwall, Truro.]*

This page upper: *Jumbo's* steam winch provides the only power to drag her reluctant charge into the Abbey basin. Hardly a 'fair lead' for hauling. Note one of the open timber gates to the dry dock on the right. *[Pawlyn/Holman Collection/Royal Institution of Cornwall, Truro.]*

Above: Docking the *Stainburn.* This dark print, made from a poor original negative, illustrates the tight access to the Holman's Dry Dock. *[Pawlyn/Holman Collection/Royal Institution of Cornwall, Truro.]*

With her successful docking the main drama closed. It now became a routine job to survey the damage, ascertain the repairs necessary and execute the work. Only one question remained to be answered, would the repairs now made be temporary or permanent? As the 'Cornishman' newspaper reported on the following Saturday -
'The s.s. *Stainburn* which we reported last week as having run on the Runnel Stone, was successfully docked on Friday afternoon, by Messrs. N. Holman and Sons, Ltd., and on Saturday morning the surveyors examined her bottom, where it was found that one plate had a large hole through it, one of the frames broken, and two keel plates so badly scored as to necessitate their being renewed. Tenders for the temporary repairs and also for completely carrying out the whole work were asked for, and we are pleased to state that the price for undertaking the whole of the work, which was submitted by Messrs. N. Holman and Sons, Ltd., was accepted. The result of the tender is specially gratifying, as not only did the price asked come under consideration, but also the time that it was estimated would be required for completing the contract. The surveyor for the underwriters expressed his pleasure that the work could be carried out locally, as he was informed before leaving Liverpool that he would be unable to get anything done at Penzance, as there was no firm capable of undertaking the work. We understand also that one of the owners of the vessel stated that if a good job was done it would mean other work to follow, which, if realised, will bring employment and money into the town.'
The closing sentences of this report encapsulated the hopes and aspirations of the firm, but unfortunately their surviving ledgers do not cover the period when the *Stainburn* was in dock, so we have no indication of the actual cost of the repairs.
Working with relatively crude machinery and equipment, then predominantly hand-powered, the semi-skilled workforce set about cutting out the damaged frames and plates. Using these to create wooden patterns, replacement frames and plates were cut, machined and worked into the required shapes. Into these the lines of rivet holes were punched out with a fairly primitive but effective punching machine. The prepared frames and plates were then

Above: Punching rivet holes in hull plates at Holman's Dry Dock. Although there is some mechanical power, supplied by an overhead belt drive, the operation is labour intensive - employing nine or ten men. Note: the vessel in the dock is not the *Stainburn*. [Pawlyn/Holman Collection/Royal Institution of Cornwall, Truro.]

Below: A quick lick of paint was applied while the repairs were effected. Note all the life belts are removed from their ready-use mounts across the bridge front. [Pawlyn/Holman Collection/Royal Institution of Cornwall, Truro.]

offered into place and riveted home. In a relatively short time the essential repairs were effected. While these were underway her owners took the opportunity to put her through a Lloyd's Survey,

giving their little steamer a general overhaul, and a quick lick of paint to freshen her up. In all she was in dry dock for 15 days, and it is intriguing that, while subsequent editions of 'Lloyd's Register of Shipping' note her as having been surveyed at Penzance in March 1906, there is no mention of any damage repairs having been then effected!

Whatever, a complete repair was effected, and on the afternoon of Saturday, 20th March she was duly undocked and hauled out to a berth alongside the back of the north wall of the floating dock. Here her 400-ton cargo of coal was re-loaded. After all the reports of her accident and repair, no report seems to have survived of precisely when she sailed from Penzance for Great Yarmouth. A quick search of subsequent 'Lloyd's Lists' has revealed no further reports on the *Stainburn*, neither of her sailing from Penzance, nor yet of her arrival at Yarmouth: a passage which should only have taken a couple of days, as indicated by that of the *Adelheid,* Sobing, which left Yarmouth for Newlyn on 3rd April and arrived on the 5th.

Re-loading probably took a few days, and when she steamed out of Penzance she was well down to her marks. Her return to sea closed one of those innumerable little incidents so common in the lives of these little ships and their crews, but aside from the cost of dry-docking and repairs, there remained the question of recompense for services rendered.

Damages for salvage

No voluntary agreement having been reached between the parties - the pilots, fishermen, owners and underwriters - there followed a court action to recover damages for salvage on the part of those going to the steamer's aid. This case was duly heard at Truro on Tuesday 2nd May and much of the foregoing account is reconstructed from the evidence then presented before Judge Grainger.

The actual damage sustained by the *Stainburn* in striking the Runnelstone was then stated as being confined to two damaged plates, and one hole comprising a gash of less than a foot. However, the value of the property at risk was assessed at £5,650 for the *Stainburn* herself, along with her cargo of coals val-

ued at £333. On the other hand the Lowestoft steam drifter *Ludham Castle* - built at Appledore in 1904 - was valued at £2,220 and her fishing gear at £400.

As might be expected there was much conflicting evidence, with Captain Little trying to play down any danger and his state of excitement and confusion. Vingoe was regarded as having given cool clear evidence, and the evidence of Newlyn Harbour Master, Thomas Oats Strick, in which he stated that when he first saw Captain Little he 'was so agitated as to be unable to keep his temper' did little for the captain's reputation. In his summing up Judge Grainger said 'he had no difficulty in coming to the conclusion that Vingoe's evidence was substantially correct. In making that statement he did not mean to say that the master of the *Stainburn* had endeavoured to mislead the Court.' But, 'it appeared that the master was pleased to find someone to take the responsibility off his shoulders'.

Counsel for the steamer's owners then tried to move that the steamer had been in no material danger, and therefore no question of salvage arose. However, when the judge pointed out that 'although the vessel might not have been in actual danger, it was in distress' counsel for the defence offered £50 in settlement. His honour thought 'the vessel was in considerable danger,' and gave judgement of £130 in favour of the salvors, of which £40 was for the services of the steam drifter. And there the matter closed.

A final fatal encounter

Unfortunately our little steamer did not continue to serve in the British coastal trade for very long. Not quite five years after her encounter with the rocks of the Runnelstone, the *Stainburn* was again ashore, and this time she was not so lucky.

On 2nd February 1911, while on a voyage from Cardiff to St. Brieuc with coal, she struck fast on the Grande Lejon rock, and her crew took to their boat and landed safely at Pleherel, La Fresnaye Bay, near St. Malo. News of her plight was picked up by the Western Marine Salvage Company, whose steamer *Lady of the Isles* was sent to try and get her off. However, a 'Lloyd's List' report dated 8th February stated that she was then :

'... lying on Bignon Rock, 16 m W. of St. Malo, 3 miles off the land, heading W. 45° list to starboard and at low water the forecastle dry, vessel 3 parts submerged, water halfway up the mizzen mast, exposed to all points of the compass. Local authorities say will dry at spring tides. Consider if weather remains fine with prompt action chance to save the vessel; weather fine, sea smooth.' Just four days later, with the '...vessel pounding badly, hold holed, cargo washing out. Have decided salvage hopeless. *Lady of the Isles* returned to Penzance.' All hope of commercial salvage having been given up, the *Stainburn* was abandoned as a total loss, and struck from the Workington Shipping Register.

THE STAINBURN STEAMSHIP CO. LTD.: A BRIEF HISTORY

The owners of the *Stainburn* whose misadventures off Penzance were described in the preceding feature were, like the ship itself, rather unfortunate. The modest fleet of the Stainburn Steamship Co. Ltd. of Workington had more than its fair share of losses, the company itself went bankrupt, whilst every one of the five ships it owned met violent ends.

Although somewhat overshadowed by Whitehaven, its older and once wealthier neighbour, Workington was an important port in the nineteenth century, shipping coal coastwise and to Ireland, and iron ore to Merseyside and South Wales. The local steelworks specialised in railway rails, which were shipped coastwise, often to Liverpool for export. Workington also had an important shipbuilder, Williamsons, which had moved its yard to the town from Harrington. Their yard built some of the last big iron and steel sailing ships, converting successfully to building steam coasters during the 1890s. When Williamsons could not find a buyer for one of their ships, they simply traded her themselves, and built up a substantial fleet of steam coasters registered at Workington.

Quite likely, local shipbrokers Isaac Murphy and Isaac Sandwith were well connected with the Williamsons. In 1903 they ordered a steel steamer from the yard, launched as *Stainburn*, which also gave its name to the owning company which Murphy and Sandwith floated in May 1903. Reflecting the cost of the steamer, the company's capital was modest, just £8,000 offered in equally modest £1 shares which would not beyond the means of small investors. Richard and Robert Williamson, the shipbuilders, took 400 shares each, probably as a way of securing orders for the company's steamers, four of which they built.

Several other local industries subscribed: the St. Helens Colliery and Brick Works Co. Ltd., the Millom and Askham Haematite Company, and further afield McDevette and Donnell, Londonderry coal merchants. Clearly, these concerns all had interests in shipping or receiving commodities from Workington. Nevertheless, this did not prevent the *Stainburn* from trading farther afield, often loading coal in South Wales ports, for instance.

The Stainburn company's shipowning ambitions remained modest for its first decade. With the loss of *Stainburn* off France in February 1911, a virtual repeat was ordered from Williamsons, the *Wythburn*. At 142 feet, she was ideally sized for trading around the Irish Sea, and particularly suited to serving Dublin's gas works. Like *Stainburn*, she was mortgaged, initially to the Bank of Whitehaven.

Possibly stimulated by the high freight rates earned during the First World War, the company went back to Williamsons for two further and larger steamers, delivered in May 1916 and June 1917. Alas, both *Cliburn* and *Lynburn* quickly became casualties of hostilities, not seeing service together.

New management took over soon after the First World War. Replacing Murphy and Sandwith in September 1919 was Henry Reynolds, a Whitehaven colliery manager. Reynolds had very brief experience

All shining and shipshape, the *Stainburn* puts out to sea from Penzance after completion of her emergency repairs. The close proximity of Pilot Boat No.3 suggests that the pilot did not intend taking her far beyond the harbour mouth. *[Pawlyn/Holman Collection/Royal Institution of Cornwall, Truro.]*

Retaining her original name, but now in the colours of Monroe Brothers, *Wythburn* enters Preston Dock during the 1930s. Like many steam coasters, she retains an open wheelhouse. *[J. and M. Clarkson]*

of ship management. His company, the Whitehaven Colliery Co. Ltd., had bought the steamer *Skernahan* (530/1902) from Howdens of Larne in January 1916, only to lose her in collision in August that year.

With only *Wythburn* surviving for the Stainburn company, a further ship was sought after the First World War, and with many builders having full order books the company went to a new yard, the Olderfleet Shipyard of William Adam and Co. at Larne Harbour. The second *Stainburn* was only the northern Irish yard's second, and also its last, completion. This *Stainburn* suffered because of the high freight rates and hence strong demand for steamers following the First World War, and her price would have been several times that of her namesake of 18 years earlier. This was probably a level of debt which the little company could not bear, as when freight rates fell they did so dramatically, and stayed down almost until the next war. In August 1928 a meeting of the Stainburn Steamship Company's shareholders agreed the melancholy conclusion that, 'by reason of its liabilities, the company cannot continue trading' and so the company was wound up. Its debtors did not wait for its affairs to be put in order. The District Bank foreclosed on the mortgage of *Wythburn* in October and on that of *Stainburn* in March 1929. The former was sold to Liverpool shipowner Kenneth R. Monroe, and the *Stainburn* to well-known Guernsey owner Onesimus Dorey. Whilst the *Wythburn* continued trading around the Irish Sea for Monroe Brothers the larger *Stainburn,* now renamed *Perelle,* probably ran largely with coal for the greenhouses of Guernsey.

During the Second World War both steamers came to violent ends. *Wythburn* was mined off Barry in October 1940, whilst *Perelle* was cut down by a US troopship in St George's Channel during March 1942. War, therefore, directly or indirectly contributed to the loss of four of the five Stainburn company's steamers.

Fleet list

1. STAINBURN (1)   1904-1911
O.N. 95408   405g   109n   141.5 x 24.0 x 10.9 feet
C. 2-cyl. by Ross and Duncan, Glasgow; 60 NHP, 525 IHP, 10 knots.
12.1903: Launched by R. Williamson and Son, Workington (Yard No.192).
13.1.1904: Registered in the ownership of the Stainburn Steamship Co. Ltd., Workington as STAINBURN.
1.1904: Completed.
4.2.1911: Foundered off Grand Lejon whilst on a voyage from Cardiff to St. Brieuc with coal.
24.2.1911: Register closed.

2. WYTHBURN   1911-1929
O.N. 128970   420g   161n   141.6 x 24.3 x 11.0 feet
C. 2-cyl. by Ross and Duncan, Govan; 83.4 NHP, 400 IHP, 9 knots.
9.1911: Launched by R. Williamson and Son, Workington (Yard No.213).
25.10.1911: Registered in the ownership of the Stainburn Steamship Co. Ltd., Workington as WYTHBURN.
16.10.1928: Sold by mortgagees to Kenneth R. Monroe, Liverpool.
29.1.1931: Transferred to Monroe Brothers Ltd.
1.12.1936: Transferred to the Kyle Shipping Co. Ltd. (Monroe Brothers, managers), Liverpool.
12.10.1937: Transferred to the Walton Steamship Co. Ltd. (F.L. Dawson and Co. Ltd., manager), Newcastle-upon-Tyne.
28.10.1940: Mined and sunk off Barry in position 51.22.30 north by 03.15 west whilst on a voyage from Buncrana to Bristol with a cargo of bog ore. Five of her crew of eight were lost.
14.2.1941: Register closed.

3. CLIBURN   1916
O.N. 133264   440g 174n   149.8 x 24.6 x 10.0 feet
T. 3-cyl. by William Beardmore and Co. Ltd., Glasgow; 83 NHP, 600 IHP, 9.5 knots.
5.1916: Completed by R. Williamson and Son, Workington (Yard No.226).
20.5.1916: Registered in the ownership of the Stainburn Steamship Co. Ltd., Workington as CLIBURN.
20.10.1916: Sunk by explosive charges placed on board by the German submarine UB 18 thirty miles south south east of St. Catherines Point whilst on a voyage from Swansea to Honfleur with a cargo of coal.
7.11.1916: Register closed.

4. LYNBURN   1917
O.N. 133265   587g 224n   165.7 x 26.6 x 11.0 feet
T. 3-cyl. by William Beardmore and Co. Ltd., Glasgow; 87.5 NHP, 500 IHP, 9 knots.
6.1917: Completed by R. Williamson and Son, Workington (Yard No.225).
27.6.1917: Registered in the ownership of the Stainburn Steamship Co. Ltd., Workington as LYNBURN.

29.8.1917: Mined and sunk half a mile south east of the North Arklow Light Vessel whilst on a voyage from Cork to Whitehaven with a cargo of pitwood.
10.11.1917: Register closed.

5. STAINBURN (2)   1922-1929
O.N. 134945   659g 265n   177.0 x 28.1 x 10.9 feet
T. 3-cyl. by Campbell and Calderwood Ltd., Paisley; 97 NHP, 630 BHP, 700 IHP, 10 knots.
4.1922: Completed by William Adam and Co. at the Olderfleet Shipyard, Larne Harbour (Yard No. 2).
8.4.1922: Registered in the ownership of the Stainburn Steamship Co. Ltd., Whitehaven as STAINBURN.
8.3.1929: Sold by the mortgagees to Cecil Dorey, Guernsey.
8.4.1929: Renamed PERELLE.
6.5.1929: Transferred to Onesimus Dorey, Guernsey.
11.11.1931: Transferred to Onesimus Dorey and Sons Ltd., Guernsey.
15.3.1942: Sunk following a collision with the troop transport U.S.S. BARNETT (9,750d/1928) five miles south of the Mull of Kintyre whilst on a voyage from Londonderry to Cardiff with a cargo of potatoes.
1.4.1942: Register closed.

Above: The second *Stainburn* in the ownership of the Stainburn Steamship Co. Ltd.   Like others in the coal trade, the company had a simple, rather sombre livery, with brown superstructure and a black funnel. Design of steam coasters had changed little since her predecessor was built in 1904, and one of the few differences apparent are shorter topmasts. Sails are still carried. *[Whitehaven Museum]*

Right: The *Stainburn* after her enforced sale by the District Bank, her mortgagees, to Onesimus Dorey of Guernsey, for whom she was renamed *Perelle*, and given a somewhat brighter livery, despite continuing largely in the coal trade. *[Roy Griffin]*

PUTTING THE RECORD STRAIGHT

Letters, additions, amendments and photographs relating to articles in any issues of *Record* are welcomed. Letters may be lightly edited. Communications by e-mail are welcome, but senders are asked to include their postal address.

Points from past issues
In 'Record' 2, page 109, you refer to the *Halladale* being scrapped as *Ferrymar* at Aruba around 1987. I saw *Ferrymar* partly dismantled in a scrap yard at Curacao in 1981. I visited Aruba and Curacao on the *Tambu Express* which ran from Miami to the Caribbean. I know of no scrap yard in Aruba at the time.
RICHARD JOLLIFFE, 54 Glendale Avenue, Wash Common, Newbury, Berkshire RG14 6RU.

I have just finished reading your superb article on Liberty ships - both in illustration and content ('In a Liberty ship engine room' by David Aris, 'Record' 24). It was especially interesting to me as I served on the *Samdel* in Far Eastern waters and the *Samakron* in the Caribbean, both during the war.
The Liberties were so alike that officers going back aboard after a night ashore would get the ships mixed up and try to get their heads down in the corresponding cabin in the wrong vessel. They had running iced water in the alleyways which the good old British shipowners immediately switched off lest British seamen got the wrong ideas.
JOANNA GREENLAW, 59 King Edward Road, Swansea SA1 4LN

Having read the article in 'Record' 26 concerning the stranding of *Innisagra* I believe the story of how and why is not geographical correct. Firstly, it is impossible to anchor beneath the Forth Bridge - the tides are too strong, and why do so 15 miles west of Kirkcaldy? I suspect it was Kirkcaldy Bay she anchored, where you cannot even see the Bridge ! Secondly, if she was being driven up the Forth (presumably by a strong north-east wind), she would have been driven up passed Bo'ness, going further away from Kirkcaldy and no chance of seeing Kinghorn. These facts rather confirm that she anchored in Kirkcaldy Bay and in the wind was driven south west finding herself off Kinghorn where there is a small sheltered beach. Kirkcaldy Bay is very exposed to north-easterly winds and really the only place for shelter for a small vessel is in the lee of Inchkeith.
Interesting little ships especially the ones with the bridge on the forecastle.
GRAEME SOMNER, 2 Farm Lane, Mudeford, Christchurch, Dorset BH23 4AH.

Phil Thomas and I think the *Frideborg* ('Record' 28) may have had her figurehead destroyed in a collision and money was not wasted in replacing it. In the photograph on page 221 the lamp screen is supported by the usual iron stanchions (clearly seen in the photographs) and out from the shrouds. I think the lamps were taken into the lamp room by the lamp trimmer each day for refilling and then put out again at dusk.
Referring to page 257, J. and C. Harrison 'sold' their colliers to William Cory in 1896, retaining bunkering operations, and became shipowners again in 1905 and had 18 ships by 1911 (see 'British Ocean Tramps', volume 2, page 105). On the same page, the *Cabo Silleiro* photograph, the barrels are *on* the hatch covers: the timber piled round the hatches gives a false impression. On page 259, *Jacinto Verdaguer* has a spoon-shaped 'teapot' bow (see 'British Ocean Tramps', volume 2, page 73). It is just part of the steel work and she would have retained it.
CHARLES WAINE, Mount Pleasant, Beamish Lane, Albrighton, Wolverhampton WV7 3JJ

With reference to 'Record' 29, page 47, there was an *Anatoliy Serov* lost by mine in the Black Sea in 1949. However, it was not the former John Holt steamer, but rather a motor vessel of 3,925 grt, built 1933, as *Kollektivizatsia*, which had been re-named *Anatoliy Serov* in 1939. She was mined and sunk on 8th April 1949 near Sevastopol. Since the 'Soviet Shipping Register' was then a restricted publication, this name change never appeared in 'Lloyd's Register'. It is not at all surprising that the reports of the loss which reached Western ears were equated with the steamer which was known.
BILL SCHELL, 334 South Franklin Street, Holbrook, MA 02343, USA

***Canadian Star*: a survivor's tale**
Congratulations as usual for 'Record', but especially for issue 29 that carries the Blue Star tale by Captain Kinghorn. What memories! The photo (page 44) of the *Canadian Star* in March 1943 is the first I've seen of a ship in convoy HX 229. Flagged as number 33, she was third (and last) ship in the third of eleven columns of the convoy; her station was thus abeam to port of the Shell tanker *Nicania* (my lot), number 83 at the tail of the eighth column.
Canadian Star was torpedoed after ten other ships, when the second column of the convoy had been wiped out but none of the third. If she had to 'sheer off to starboard' avoiding a stricken ship, as per Captain Kinghorn's surmise, someone had to be out of position, as was quite normal in those fateful hours of the convoy's dodging, perplexing historians British or German. Indeed, a Liberty ship that regained position after a convoy manoeuvre in the blackout affords me time alive to record these facts. After heavy attack on the starboard wing of the convoy, the Dutch *Zaanland* (number 103) fell back sinking, exposing the tanker *Nicania*. From the same salvo by U 758 one 'eel' would have blown *Nicania* sky high, had it not been stopped instead by the Liberty ship *James Ogilvie* (number 93) finding her due place in time to save us lunatics who hazarded all a patriot may. The young third mate of *Nicania* chalked a mark on the course board in the wheelhouse for every thump all around us, which could mean a ship murdered in the dark. Scoring 16 before the change of watch, he might have tallied the Navy's depth charges to guard our floating bomb. Then in the graveyard watch, 12 to 4, salvoes from U 91 and U 600 sank half the ships left on the convoy's starboard wing, but it happened that one torpedo crossed our bow to hit the *Southern Princess* (number 72) on our port hand. Flaming, she made a duly brilliant beacon to silhouette our tanker (number 83) as we ambled past her on a dawning St. Patrick's Day. A whaling ship in this war, she had been the super tanker *San Patricio* of 1917.
Perhaps one (or more) of the 40 U-boats spared *Nicania* because we looked so foolish, with our net booms high in the air like maypoles while torpedoes hied every which way below. This tanker (new in 1942) was forbidden to stream torpedo nets in convoy HX 229, lest we lessen by two knots the ten-knot speed of ships in company, pitted against U-boats easily making 18 knots.
As for 'sheer off to starboard' when the ship ahead is hit, this is just what saved lives in *Lafian* when the commodore's *John Holt* was torpedoed on 24th September 1941. With our altering course the *Lafian* took the torpedo of U 107 not in the engine room but in number 4 hold, spraying palm kernels high on the monkey island.
GERALD MORGAN, 601 Bellevue Tower, 195 Twenty-First Street, West Vancouver, B.C. Canada V7V 4A4

***Polaris*' prequel**
I greatly enjoyed Anthony Cooke's article on the early ships of the Finland Line in 'Record 28', but by coincidence needed to check the history of the Russian *Sestroretsk* which had started life in 1912 as *Prinzessin Sophie Charlotte* before

becoming *Preussen* in 1922 and then *Polaris* (2) from 1933 until becoming *Sestroretsk* as part of the post-war reparations ... all as listed by Anthony Cooke. However, the Starke Schell Register for 1912 indicates that this ship had an earlier life under the Russian flag, being seized at Petrograd in August 1914 and enlisted as an Imperial Russian Navy transport named *Rcy* (I wonder if that has been correctly translated from Cyrillic?). In the following month she became *Ilmen*, operating as a minelayer from June 1915. On 7th April 1918 she was captured by the German *Moewe* south of Abo, and became an Imperial German Navy submarine depot ship from May 1918 until returning to her pre-war owners and name in January 1919.
GEORGE ROBINSON, Southwood Cottage, 79 Southwood Road, Cottingham HU16 5AJ

Minding our Bs and Ds
Knowing how much you try to be accurate, and not having seen a correction, (I don't have issue 28 yet so ignore this if already done) I must correct the caption for *Benvannoch* on page 63 of 'Record' 25. She is very obviously a 'B' type, not a 'D' as in the caption. Mitchell and Sawyer seem to have had a rare lapse here. The 'B' class had the big gap between bridge and funnel, the 'D' class had a composite superstructure with three hatches forward and two aft and a half height poop, but since they had bulwarks rather than rails this poop was not particularly evident. The 'C' type was very similar but with a full height poop. Incidentally, does anyone know why two types, the 'C' and 'D', apparently identical apart from the poop, were built during the war? It seems to

unnecessarily complicate things.
Congratulations on a continuing magnificent series.
DAVE EDGE, 69 Onslow Street, Bluff, New Zealand

Nicknames from Wales
I saw Alan Phipps' letter on nicknames in the latest 'Record', so I thought I'd add a few that I've heard over the years - it might make a nice sequel to 'Poetry Corner'.
The three dirty R's - Radcliffe, Ropner and Runciman. Radcliffe was also known as the 'Cardiff British India Line', having identical funnel markings.
After Evans and Reid bought Radcliffe's in 1947, they adopted a yellow chevron funnel mark, and soon became known as the 'Boy Scout Line'.
The three dirty S's - Smith, Strick and Seager.
Was not Ropner's funnel mark called 'the old bread and jam'?
Ropner's 'next' ship - the *Cesspool*.
Chapman's 'next' ship - the *Skeleton*.
In Cardiff, Chapman's were called 'the envelope boats', from their funnel mark, and Houlder's 'the Grange boats', from their names.
Richard Hughes's fleet was also called the 'Welsh navy', and of course the 'Rose boats'. Do I recall that you had heard of 'Hungry Dick' too?
And a few in Welsh!
The ships of the great sailing fleet operated by the Davies brothers of Menai Bridge were called *llongau un aderyn* (one bird ships) because so little rubbish was thrown over the stern - no matter how rotten the food, the crew had to

Only the slightest excuse, provided by David Jenkins letter, is needed for one of the editors to feature a ship from his favourite coaster company, Richard Hughes of Liverpool. This recently-acquired photograph, possibly by one of the River Ouse photographers, shows the Dutch-built *Blush Rose* of 1913. The grey hull was very unusual for a Hughes ship in peacetime, and suggests she is almost new. This is confirmed by the sails, tightly furled against the masts - these were supplied when a steam coaster was new but rarely replaced when they wore out.

A Welshman himself, born in Gronant on the north coast, Richard Hughes recruited many of his crews from Anglesey, and in particular the village of Moelfre, hence the 'Welsh Navy' nickname for his fleet. The sobriquet 'Hungry Dick' was no more deserved than similar nicknames for other owners, such as 'Hungry Hogarths'. When times were good in the coasting trade, crews often received more than the going rate. Conversely, when they were bad - as they were right through the 1920s and 1930s - wages were reduced, a crude profit sharing unpopular with unions.

Although he never went hungry, Hughes did not grow rich from his shipowning. Gambling that the

depression of the 1920s would soon be over, he indulged in a major building programme - 11 relatively large ships delivered in just 18 months. But the recession merely deepened into depression, his creditors foreclosed, and Hughes' company went into receivership. It was an indication of Hughes' stature in coastal shipping, however, that new management kept his name and other details, although enforcing a rigid regime of economy.

Blush Rose survived into this new phase of the company's history, after 1934 being owned by Richard Hughes and Co. (Liverpool) Ltd., although Cardiff shipbroker Thomas Tierney was now managing director. *Blush Rose* also survived the Second World War, although she had a few anxious hours in February 1942 when an attack by the Luftwaffe off St Ann's Head, Pembrokeshire led to her being beached in Dale Roads. Her end came on 2nd August 1945, when an unequal encounter with Alfred Holt's *Glaucus* (7,586/1921) led to her sinking about 20 miles off Holyhead during a ballast passage from Dublin to Preston.

Anyone wishing to know more about Hughes is directed to 'Mersey Rovers', excellent value for a 344-page hardback at £15 plus postage from Ships in Focus.

eat it!

Llongau Aberystwyth (the ships of Aberystwyth) - John Mathias and Sons. Also called 'the College Line', because they named their ships after public schools.

Llongau Pwllparc (the Pwllparc ships) - Owen and Watkin Williams, after the brothers' native farm near Edern.

DAVID JENKINS, Senior Curator, Department of Industry National Museums and Galleries of Wales.

Nicknames from elsewhere

When I was with Ben Line they were always known as 'Leith Greeks' due to their propensity for buying old ships and ekeing a few more years work out of them.

Wijne & Barends, the Dutch coaster fleet, have a W&B on their funnel, and is known as 'water and bread', initials which fit both English and Dutch versions.

BARRY STANDERLINE, Kia-ora, Herds Crescent, Johnshaven, Montrose DD10 0EZ

Spanish intelligence

As a Spanish enthusiast, I would like to comment on 'Spying on Spain: 2' in 'Record' 28.

Cabo Roche and *Cabo Silleiro* both spent their long commercial lives (42 and 49 years respectively) working on their owners' short sea route around Spain carrying general cargo, a service closely knitted with that of Aznar Line under the banner 'Mancomunadas del Cabotaje.'

Ea went into the ownership of Maria M. Menendez Ponte under the same name before being renamed *Somio* and broken up here in Santander.

Capitan Segarra before being broken up became the headquarters of the Sea Masters association in Bilbao, and also a second office for most of the shipbroker members of the Bilbao association Consulado de Bilbao.

Ita as *España No.1* was part of a group of six which were seized by the Spanish Government after the First World War as reparation for Spanish tonnage sunk by German U-boats. All had been interned in Spanish ports and after seizure were allocated by the Government to shipping companies which had lost units to enemy action.

The other vessels seized were:

España No.2 (3,919/1908) built at Hoboken as *Javorina* and allocated to Compañia Transmediterránea and renamed *Generalife*.

España No.3 (2,108/1906) built in Rostock as *Roma* and allocated to Empresa Nacional Elcano as *Castillo Figueras*.

España No.4 (3,829/1895) built at Stettin as *Crefeld*

and allocated to Trasmediterránea as *Teide*.

España No.5 (2,156/1906) built at Lübeck as *Riga* and allocated to Empresa Nacional Elcano as *Castillo Tordesillas*.

España No.6 (5,519/1901) built at Newcastle was originally named *Neuenfels* by Hansa and was allocated to the Spanish Navy to be rebuilt as a seaplane carrier and renamed *Dedalo*.

El Condada and *El Montecillo* were owned by Compañia General de Navegacion SA of Barcelona and the management of Alejandro Navajas (a well established owner of wine cellars at La Rioja). I believe only one shareholder of the company is still alive, living in Santander and well into his nineties.

Jacinto Verdaguer was formerly *Cid* of Compañia Maritima SA, Barcelona, a Spanish offshoot of Macandrews and Company, owning fruit carriers under the Spanish flag. This company sold out in 1918 and their fleet went to Compañia Transmediterránea when this company was set up.

Another vessel of the same origin went to Transmediterránea, *Velazquez* (1,344/1902) built by the Clyde Shipbuilding and Engineering Co. Ltd. at Port Glasgow, later renamed *Torras y Bages* and not broken up until 1966. Three other units of the fleet which went to Transmediterránea became *Juan Maragall*, *Roger de Flor* and *Rius y Taulet*.

Jaime Gerona: the actual name was *Jaime Girona* after a Catalonian businessman who was a partner of the Ybarra family (owners of iron ore mines, regular suppliers of British firms such as Consett Iron for many years).

Jose Tartiere's former names were *Josefa* and *Tomasin*, never *Genarin*.

Mar Negro. I took a photograph of her leaving Santander Bay in the sixties showing her to be one of the most beautiful vessels ever built in this country: an opinion shared by many Spanish shiplovers. She came into the fleet of a Santander owner who renamed her *Rio Pisueña*. As *Mar Negro* she always traded from Spain to the Gulf of Mexico and US East Coast ports under the banner of Maritima del Nervion SA (Urquijo and Aldecoa, managers). The Aldecoa family had a wonderful collection of oil paintings of vessels owned by themselves which was stolen some years ago.

FERNANDO DE BASTERRECHEA, Hijos de Basterrechea SA, C/Juan de Herrera No.2, 39002 Santander, Spain.

Señor Basterrechea has kindly contributed further details to the fourth 'Spying on Spain' feature in this issue.

FROM THE BOSUN'S LOCKER
John Clarkson

01/30 Bosun's Locker opens with a request from Ian Wilson to identify the location of this shot of the steam coaster *Nora*. Built at Bowling in 1906 for Joseph Monks of Liverpool, she passed to the Monroe family in 1925. She is almost certainly in Monroe colours in this shot, and this dates it between 1925 and 23rd November 1938, when *Nora* was wrecked at the entrance to Loch Ryan whilst on a voyage from Girvan to Creetown in ballast. The little steamer - *Nora* was only 100 feet long and 226 tons gross - often traded to the tiny harbours of the Solway Firth, and this as well as Ireland is a possible location

02/30 A *Carte Postale* but with no indication as to the country of origin. The ship is not named but can be identified as *Calanda*, completed in 1898 by Charles Connell and Company at Glasgow as the *Knight Errant* for the Knight Steam Ship Co. Ltd. (Greenshields, Cowie and Co.) of Liverpool. She later held the names *Rio Tiete* and *Omsk* before taking the name *Calanda* in 1921 when purchased by the London Steamship and Trading Corporation Ltd. (W.J.M.Bell), London. She held the name for only two years before being sold and renamed *Flackwell* and later *Lancing* when she was converted to a whale factory, surviving until April 1942 when torpedoed and sunk. (See 'Record' 6, pages 92-3). There is no problem as to the name of the ship but what is the barge alongside her for, or what is it loaded with, and where was the picture taken? We have enlarged a small section for easier examination.

03/30 What is the name of the tanker aground, with a serious list and receiving assistance from a salvage vessel converted from a 'Kil' class gunboat ? The only clue to the whereabouts may be a note on the back: *Included in the original collection of Gerald Brown, King Edward VI School, Totnes, Devon.*

First of all it is with deep regret that I have to report the passing of two strong supporters of Ships in Focus - W.A.(Bill) Laxon in New Zealand, author and regular correspondent and Dennis H.Johnzon here in the UK, author of the articles in Record 29 and 30 on Furness-Houlder. Ian Farquhar has written about Bill and I feel we can do no better than publish his words verbatim.

William Allan Laxon - 1937-2005

New Zealand's most prolific maritime researcher and writer has died. Bill Laxon of Whangateau, north of Auckland passed away on 15th October after a long illness. He was 68. Admitted to the Auckland bar in 1959 he had a distinguished law career and retired as one of the senior partners in Brookfields in 1997. He remained a consultant until 2003. He was well respected in Auckland legal circles and was awarded an MBE in 1988 for his work for Presbyterian Support, the social service arm of the Presbyterian Church. His interest in ships and shipping history was generated by his grandfather, who was an engineer with the Northern Steam Ship Company, and often took his grandson down to his coastal steamer at the Auckland wharves. Bill soon developed an intense interest in ships and at the age of 17 he contributed his first article to New Zealand Marine News and has been a continuous writer for the journal ever since. He wrote the occasional article for Sea Breezes, and also for the first and second series of The Log based in Melbourne. His publications include Asiatic Steam Navigation Co. Ltd. 1878-1963 (1963), Steamers Down the Firth (1966), Steam on the Manukau (1966), The Shire Line (1972), The Straits Steamship Fleet 1890-1975 (with R.K. Tyers) (1975), Nourse Line (with Fred Perry) (1991), B.I. The British India Steam Navigation Co. Ltd. (with Fred Perry) (1994), Davey of the Awatea (1997), Crossed Flags – New Zealand. Shipping Company and Federal Steam Navigation Company and their subsidiaries (with Ian Farquhar, Nigel Kirby and Fred Perry) (1997), The Currie Line of Melbourne (2003) and The Straits Steamship Fleets (2004). An updated and expanded history of his Shire Line history is being published in 2005. In addition he has helped many other writers with their own publications and exchanged information with a network of correspondents around the world. He was one of the founders of the Auckland Maritime Society in 1957, an Honorary Vice President of the N.Z. Ship and Marine Society for 46 years and was a member of the World Ship Society for over 50 years. A founding Trustee of the Auckland Maritime Museum in 1981, he played a significant role in the development of the Museum which in recent years has become the New Zealand National Maritime Museum and has also achieved a measure of financial viability. The Auckland Branch of the Company of Master Mariners made him an honorary member and his long time involvement with the Auckland War Memorial Museum saw him being made a Companion of the Museum in 2003. A stickler for detail and accuracy, he was often critical of those who were careless with the facts, but the high standards he set encouraged others to do likewise. His extensive knowledge of shipping history will be sorely missed.

Roy and I agree completely with what Ian writes and we shall certainly miss Bill's contributions to Putting the Record Straight, some may say nit-picking, but essential to Record where we strive for 100% accuracy. Our sympathies go to Lorna, his wife and to all his family.

Dennis Johnzon - 1922-2004

Well known for his expertise on Houlders, Dennis Johnzon died in December 2004. Born in Tottenham, north east London, Dennis was the eldest of three brothers and after attending boarding school was apprenticed to Houlders, his first ship being the *Hardwicke Grange* of 1921. His personal knowledge of Houlder ships and men was reflected in his writing, including his work on the Furness-Houlder meat ships, currently appearing in Record and which, sadly, he did not live to see into print. After serving with Houlders throughout the war, he left on getting married and became a sales representative. Besides ships, his great interest was classical music, although sadly he lost his hearing about four years ago.

Post-war, Dennis became Houlder's unofficial archivist, also taking a great interest in their parent, Furness Withy. Dennis was an assiduous researcher, pursuing information on his chosen ships until the very end. At the time of his final illness, he was searching for a report on a diving expedition on a Houlder war loss off the east coast. Dennis was also a great letter writer, and never satisfied until a sheet of paper was filled with his closely-spaced typing.

We at Ships in Focus will miss Dennis's enthusiasm, knowledge and generosity with his information, and are pleased to have been able to publish his comprehensive work on Furness-Houlder. The final resting place of his extensive collection of Houlder data and photographs has yet to be settled, although at least one museum is expressing interest. We extend our sympathy to Dennis' wife and his two sons and one daughter.

Whilst completing this article I have just been advised of the death on Sunday 13th February 2005 of Derek Blackhurst, author of Philip & Son Ltd., Shipbuilders & Engineers, published by Ships in Focus in 2001. Our deepest sympathies go to his wife Margaret and daughter Gillian. A full obituary will be included in Record 31.

Photographs for identification

We received a number of responses to the photos published in Record 29 and we are now confident of the identity of two of the ships. Soon after we went to press Sea Breezes featured several views of the ship depicted in 01/29. There is no doubt that our picture is a further view of the Italian *Ausonia* (12,995/1928). Owned by Lloyd Triestino she caught fire following an explosion on 18th October 1935 at Alexandria. Beached in Ramleh Bay on 18th/19th Ausonia became a constructive total loss, was sold and towed to Pola in December 1935 to be broken up.

Unknown to me picture 02/29 has appeared on the Riversea and Tugtalk websites in the not too distant past and the consensus is that the tug is the *Flying Foam* built in 1877 by Napier and Murray Ltd. at Port Glasgow. There is a distant view of her in the book The Clyde Shipping Company, Glasgow 1815 to 2000 (page 62) but looks much different having only one mast ahead of the engine room casing with her funnel in the usual position. Re-boilering in 1883 may account for the change in appearance. There is also a photo of her in Phil Thomas's British Steam Tugs and here she looks similar to 02/29. Not being in Clyde or Lawson colours one assumes she is at Belfast in the period 1889 to 1900. The copings on the quay are unusually painted so perhaps someone may be able to make a positive link with this or with her pale funnel.

Although we have not come up with a name for 03/29, John Naylon has pointed much out to us about the ship. She is a French barquentine employed in the cod fishery on the Grand Banks, one of the enormous fleet based on the ports in the Gulf of St Malo. She has evidently been in a collision and lost all her headgear which has brought down her foremast above the lower topsail yard. The prudent Bretons have salvaged all the spars by lashing them to the rigging. A dory, used for catching the cod by line, can be seen on top of the deckhouse at the foot of the foremast and another is just visible behind the rigging of the main mast. The trade ended with the start of the war in 1939. The name of the ship remains a mystery but perhaps some day someone will come across the same print which will have been named by the photographer.

There is no problem with reverting back to unknown photos in earlier issues but please quote the reference number to avoid errors or misunderstandings.

The Bristol Series

On the subject of the Bristol Series of postcards we now know they were published by Jonathan York, 15 Broad Quay, Bristol. Details of how the collection came to be split up are still sought. Can anyone supply us with the current address of Per-Erik Johnson in Norway, believed to be the recipient of the Scandinavian section of the negatives, and perhaps the last surviving person with knowledge of the disposal of the negatives?

A plea for help

United Baltic, Glen and Shire Lines, Clan Line and Ben Line are the subjects of projects for 2005. We now have good basic portrait type photos of most of the fleets, however it will add to the publications if we could include some 'out of the usual' pictures. Perhaps ships in ports not normally visited, large or unusual pieces of cargo being loaded or discharged and ships in difficult situations would be of great help. In the last category a photo of the *Clan Mackenzie* (6554/1917) sitting on the bottom at the Mersey Bar in October 1937 with her decks awash, following a collision with the *Manchester Regiment* (5989/1922) is much sought after. Photos appeared in the national press at the time but we have not yet tracked down original prints.

In the first instance please do not send original photographs, only photocopies or low resolution scans. We will contact you if we can use the photographs to request the loan of them.

Thank you to Richard Cox, Nigel Farrell, John Naylon, George Robinson and Tony Smythe for their help and interest.

SPYING ON SPAIN: 4

Roy Fenton and Fernando Basterrechea

This is a final selection of photographs of Spanish ships from a collection put together by British intelligence during 1943 and 1944. All ships featured have engines aft, either tankers or small freighters. The original prints are small and often rather closely cropped.

CAMPECHE

Soc. Espanola de Const. Navale, Cadiz; 1934, 6,382gt, 413 feet
Oil engines 2SCSA 8-cyl. by Soc. Espanola de Const. Navale, Cadiz driving twin screw

Of the 20 tankers in the Spanish fleet in 1944, 16 belonged to the state oil company, Compania Arrendataria del Monopolio de Petroleos S.A., shortened to CAMPSA, formed in 1928.

Campeche was one of five *Campas*-type tankers, which had been built for CAMPSA at various yards since 1932. Despite their tall funnels, they were diesel-driven. Seen deeply-laden on 2nd July 1944, she was unusual in carrying life rafts immediately behind her bridge. *Campeche* was in Republican hands during the Spanish Civil War, voyaging several times to the Black Sea. However, on one these voyages she struck a mine off Cape Bagur and, severely damaged, made it into Barcelona, only to be damaged further during an air attack. She was then taken to Marseilles where she was recovered in March 1939. Post-war service was long, *Campeche* being broken up at Valencia in 1969 by Aguilar y Peris.

CAMPERO

Echevarrieta y Larrinaga, Cadiz, 1934, 6,382gt, 413 feet
Oil engines 2SCSA 8-cyl. by Soc. Espanola de Const. Navale, Cadiz driving twin screws

Seen in June 1943, *Campero* was another unit of the *Campas* class. In Republican hands during the Civil War, she was returning from Constanza in the Black Sea when torpedoed by a Nationalist submarine in the Golfe du Lyon. She limped into Barcelona, and was evacuated to Marseilles. *Campero* was broken up in 1968 by Hierros Ardes S.A. at Gandia.

CAMPOAMOR

Compania Euskalduna de Const. Bilbao; 1931, 7,873gt, 455 feet
Oil engines 4SCSA 14-cyl. by Maschinenbau Augsburg-Nürnberg, Augsburg, Germany driving twin screws

The Spanish tanker fleet was relatively modern and a considerable proportion were diesel powered. Amongst the largest, *Campoamor* initially worked for the Republican Government during the Civil War, making voyages to Port Arthur and Philadelphia to Bilbao and Santander. On a third voyage from the USA, she was detained by the Nationalist auxiliary cruiser *Ciudad de Valencia*, but escaped disguised as a British tanker, the *Pollux*, and sought safety in the French port of Le Verdon. However, the escape was only temporary, as her master decided to turn her over to the Nationalists and he delivered her to Franco's forces in Pasajes during July 1937. *Campoamor* survived to be broken up in 1969 by Aguilar y Peris, Valencia.

CAMPILO

Union Navale de Levante S.A., Valencia; 1941; 3,971gt, 343 feet
Oil engines 4SCSA 12-cyl. by Maquinista Terrestre y Maritima, Barcelona driving twin screws

The motor tanker *Campilo* is one of the newest vessels featured in these 'spy' photographs, having been launched in November 1936 but the Civil War meant she was not completed until January 1941. Like the other CAMPSA tankers, she looks well cared for in this photograph taken on 28th August 1944. Indeed, the Spanish must have decided that maintaining peacetime colours, rather than painting their ships grey, was helpful in identifying them as neutrals. During the war, *Campilo* was used in short-distance trades around the Iberian Peninsula, and for bunkering. In a nice piece of symmetry, she was broken up in the port in which she was built, her demolition by Industrial e Cercial de Levante S.A. being reported in September 1972.

CAMPANARIO

R. Duncan and Co. Ltd., Port Glasgow; 1928, 5,586gt, 407 feet

T-3-cyl. by Rankin and Blackmore Ltd., Greenock.

As her Clydeside builder suggests, this steam tanker was built for British owners, Gow, Harrison and Co. also of Glasgow, as *Vallejo*. In 1937 she was sold to the Republican Government of Spain and as *Saustan* registered in the ownership of Compania Arrendataria del Monopolio de Petroleos S.A. (CAMPSA).

At the conclusion of the Civil War she was recovered at Saint Louis du Rhone, France; temporarily placed in the ownership of Gerencia de Buques Incautados and re-named *Castillo Campanario*. When her owners became Empresa Nacional Elcano, the Spanish state shipping company, the tanker was transferred back to CAMPSA, becoming simply *Campanario*.

After these eventful years, *Campanario* steamed on until 1971, when what must have been one of the very few steam-reciprocating-engined tankers still surviving was bro-ken up at Bilbao by Hierros Eduardo Varela.

REMEDIOS

Armstrong, Whitworth & Co. Ltd., Newcastle-upon-Tyne; 1921, 4,454gt, 371 feet

Oil engines 2SCSA 8-cyl. by Sulzer Frères, Winterthur, Switzerland driving twin screws

Completed as *Conde De Churruca* for Soc. Commercial de Oriente, San Sebastian, from 1927 this tanker was owned by Compañia General de Tabacos de Filipinas. This company was formed during the late 19th century when the Philippines were under Spanish control. Owners included the chairman and several directors of the Compañia Trasatlantica Espanola, and the company originally ran a cargo liner service between Liverpool and Manila via the Mediterranean, with calls at Santander on the return voyage to discharge tobacco.

In 1928 *Conde De Churruca* was incorporated into the fleet of the nationalised petroleum company, CAMPSA, who, rather than give her a name beginning with *Camp-*, renamed her *Remedios* in 1930. She spent the Civil War in Republican hands, and survived until 1958 when broken up at Barcelona by Hijo de Miguel Mateu.

CASTILLO ALMENARA

Tyne Iron Shipbuilding Co., Ltd., Newcastle-upon-Tyne; 1923, 5,387gt, 365 feet

Two steam turbines by the Wallsend Slipway and Engineering Co. Ltd., Newcastle-upon-Tyne double reduction geared to a single screw.

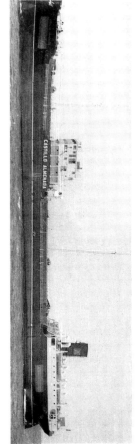

Although it is a slightly dull photograph, the life of the tanker depicted was anything but. Built as *Oilfield* for Hunting and Son, Newcastle, she was sold in 1937 to the Mid-Atlantic Shipping Co. Ltd., managed by the erstwhile ferry operators Townsend Brothers Shipping Ltd. Renamed *English Tanker* there is a strong suspicion that she was to run the Nationalist blockade into Republican-held ports. On 7th June 1938 she was discharging oil at Alicante when attacked by Nationalist aircraft. Her crew abandoned her and she subsequently sank. She was refloated on 26th April 1939 when the Nationalists had taken over, repaired and returned to service as *Castillo Almenara* in the ownership of the Spanish Government. In 1947 she was transferred to CAMPSA, who was already managing her, and her name brought into line as *Camposines*. As this she lasted until 1967 when broken up at Castellon by Desguaces Incolesa.

LOLITA ARTAZA

T. Van Duijvendijk, Lekkerkerk, Netherlands; 1925, 1,523, 246 feet

T. 3-cyl. by H. Versteeg & Zonen, Hardinxveld

The Dutch built a number of small steamers intended for the British market during the First World War when UK yards were busy with war work. However, it is unusual to find amongst them this collier, built for Harrisons (London) Colliers, Ltd., London in a Neth-erlands yard as the *Harcourt*. She was sold to Spain as *Lolita Artaza* for Artaza y Cia., San Sebastian in 1934. In 1936 she was requisitioned by the Basque Government as *Ixas Zabal*, and managed to escape the attentions of the Nationalist battle cruiser *España* in the first few months of the Civil War. She then made two voyages with iron ore to the UK before being laid up in Plymouth. She was returned to her owners and former name in 1939, and lasted until 1974 when broken up at Vigo by Martin y Oliviera.

CONDE DE ZUBIRIA

Soc. Española de Const. Naval, Bilbao; 1918, 3,308gt, 314 feet
Two steam turbines by Soc. Española de Const. Navale, Ferrol single-reduction geared to a single shaft

The engines aft, bridge amidships design was very unusual in the Spanish fleet, but was chosen for two ships in the iron ore trades. Note also the unusual position for the boats alongside the mainmast in this photograph, which was taken in August 1943.

Conde de Zubiria ran in the iron ore trade from Bilbao to UK ports until 11th March 1937 when she was intercepted off Ushant and damaged by the Republican sloop *Galerna*. She put into Brest, but her owners decided not to risk further voyages to Spain, and she traded between the UK and the Gulf of Mexico and between UK and Leningrad with scrap and timber. She was at Immingham at the end of the Civil War.

Turbine machinery was an extremely unusual choice for such a humble freighter, especially during the First World War. But it seems to have been very dependable as *Conde de Zubiria* gave fifty years of service to her one owner, Soc. Anon. Altos Hornos de Vizcaya of Bilbao. She was broken up at Bilbao 1968 by Hierros Varela, work beginning 19th February 1968.

VICTOR DE CHAVARRI

Soc. Española de Const. Naval, Bilbao; 1919, 3,308gt, 314 feet
T. 3-cyl. by Swan Hunter and Wigham Richardson Ltd., Newcastle-upon-Tyne

Photographed in August 1943. *Victor de Chavarri* was a near sister to *Conde de Zubiria* but with a more conventional reciprocating engine. However, note the large kingpost/ventilator immediately in front of the bridge. Both ships were named after company directors.

Victor de Chavarri was captured by the Nationalist destroyer *Velasco* on 30th December 1936, in the Bay of Biscay, and was used by Franco's forces as a transport. Not until the end of the Civil War was she returned to her owners, Altos Hornos de Vizcaya Soc. Anon., Bilbao. Post-war work was mainly carrying coal from Gijon to Bilbao or Sagunto, and iron ore from Sagunto to Bilbao, a trade the Spanish nicknamed 'the carousel'. *Victor de Chavarri* lasted even longer than her near sister, and in 1970 was converted into a lighter, remaining listed even in 'Lloyd's Register' into the 1990s.

ALEJANDRO No. 3

Alejandro Bengoechea y Cia. Ltda., Bilbao; 1940, 868gt, 197 feet
T. 3-cyl. Soc. Española de Const. Navale, Bilbao

Alejandro No. 3 is essentially a large steam coaster. Her owners A. Bengoechea y Urquizu (presumably a partnership including her builder) specialised in trawlers, at least after the Second World War, and there may be the suspicion that, with fishing grounds being heavily restricted during the war, they turned instead to cargo ships. Her life was short: *Alejandro No. 3* foundered on 29th November 1949 whilst on a voyage from Gijon to Malaga with a cargo of coal.

CASTILLO VERA

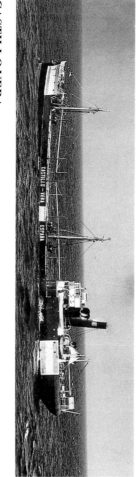

Chantiers et Atelier Aug. Normande, Le Havre; 1921, 996gt, 219 feet
T. 3-cyl. by Chantiers et Atelier Aug. Normande, Le Havre

In contrast with the previous entry, *Castillo Vera* had a remarkably complex and adventurous life. She was built as *Verrier* for the French Government, which suggests she may belong to that seriously under-recorded group, the French First World War standard ships. From 1922 to 1934 she was in the hands of various French commercial owners as *Quillebeuf*, with a short intermission from 1929 to 1931 under the Argentine flag. In 1934 an intriguing Cyprus-based outfit called the Inter Levant Steamship Co. Ltd. bought her and registered her in London as *Eleni*, a name which suggests Greek principals. They may have used her as a blockade runner, as *Eleni* was sunk by Nationalist air attack at Aguilas on 30th November 1938. When refloated in 1940 she was taken into Spanish Government ownership as *Castillo Vera*, in 1942 her owners becoming the nationalised Empresa Nacional 'Elcano' S.A., and she was photographed in their colours on 18th April 1944. In 1947 she was sold, without change of name, to a lady member of the Ponte Naya family in Corunna, but did not survive long, being wrecked on 15th February 1948 at Orriñana, near Cudillero, Asturias, whilst on a ballast voyage from her home port to San Esteban de Pravia.

TODAY'S NEWS; TOMORROW'S HISTORY

The activities of the World Ship Society encompass both the present and the past. Our monthly 64-page magazine *Marine News* provides a unique source of information on ships launched, sold, renamed, lost or broken up throughout the world. A collection of *Marine News* and their annual indexes is a vital source for anyone researching ships or shipping companies since the war.

Whilst *Marine News* is providing material for tomorrow's historians, the World Ship Society is helping today's researchers, and publishing the results of their work. The resources of our Central Record allow us to provide information on most major ships back to the 1830s and sometimes earlier. Our Photo Library is a major international collection of negatives of merchant vessels and warships. We publish the results of members' researches in high-quality books which are available to other members at privilege prices.

For details of what WSS membership can offer for an annual subscription of just £29 and a free sample copy of *Marine News* send your name and address to:- W.S.S. (SF), 101 The Everglades, Hampstead, Gillingham, Kent, ME7 3PZ, U.K.

Ships in Focus Publications
ISBN 1 901 703 76 2

£7.00

ISBN 1-901703-76-2

9 781901 703764

SHIPS IN FOCUS
RECORD
26

Ships in Focus Publications

THE LAST WORD ON A GREAT COMPANY

HARRISONS OF LIVERPOOL
A chronicle of ships and men 1830-2002
By Graeme Cubbin

For over 150 years, T. & J. Harrison was one of the great British shipping companies; successful in developing and maintaining its many trades, employing some of the best officers and crews, and building and running superb ships. *Harrisons of Liverpool* does full justice to its story. In six parts, the text gives equal coverage to the company, its ships and its men. Included is a wealth of material on events and incidents involving Harrison ships and their crews, giving a unique insight into the company, which no previous publication has matched. The fleet list covers all 333 owned and managed ships, giving extensive technical details, an account of their Harrison service, and records their subsequent lives and fates. Photographs of the majority of Harrisons' ships are included.

 Harrisons of Liverpool has been written by a former Marine Superintendent of the company, with an intimate knowledge of the company and who has enjoyed full access to its records and the memories of his colleagues. The result is a major work, which is set to be the last word on Harrisons, their ships and men, a fitting tribute to a century and a half of endeavour.

This 400-page, A4 book has hundreds of illustrations, many in colour, and represents superb value at a price to Record subscribers of £28 plus £5 postage in UK and Europe or £8 elsewhere (seamail).

ISBN 1 901703 48 7

Published jointly by the World Ship Society and Ships in Focus Publications.

Orders to Dept HL, Ships in Focus, 18 Franklands, Longton, Preston PR4 5PD, UK or ring the Ships in Focus credit card order line: 01772 612855.